PUBLISH YOUR WAY
TO MORE CLIENTS

Alexa Whitten

PUBLISH YOUR WAY TO MORE CLIENTS

ISBN 978-1-907308-07-9

Published by Compass Publishing
www.Compass-Publishing.com

Designed and Set by The Book Refinery Ltd
www.TheBookRefinery.com

Printed in the UK by P2D

What People are Saying About
'Publish Your Way to More Clients'

"Whenever I am given a 'How to' book, I am always sceptical of the claim. Will the book deliver on the promise and show me exactly 'how to' do whatever it is they claim will make me more knowledgeable, more famous, more successful, less hassled, less stressed?

So it is refreshing to read a book like this and discover exactly 'how to' do something, with a step-by-step, easy-to-follow guide.

Alexa's book takes the guesswork, pain and fear out of writing and publishing your own book. And even better, she tells you exactly what your book should be doing for you, honestly, with no soft-soaping.

What's more, she also gives you some pretty awesome tips on how to prevent expensive mistakes you may not have thought of. That alone pays dividends on the investment of buying this book.

Alexa has published my own two books and I wouldn't hesitate going back to her for my third.

Read this book, follow the steps and before too long you'll have birthed a beautiful book that will do the hard work of getting clients to your door."

Kat Smith - www.growyoursalonfast.com

Author of 'Grow Your Salon FAST: The Quick, Dirty, Uncensored Secrets to Effortless High-Street Domination Despite Cut-Throat Competition, Insane Regulation and Obnoxious Clients'

"This book is brilliant. Alexa is imparting so much terrific advice and information. You could go it alone and produce your book, BUT DON'T! Through Alexa and her team at The Book Refinery, my projects paid for themselves and if it wasn't for the ongoing support and discipline that she offered me, neither of my books would have been published and produced to such a high standard and within such a short time period. Apart from the projects paying for themselves, I continue to make a profit while getting leads that the cowboy imitations don't get near.

As a published author, I've been asked to give interviews on BBC Radio, ITV and, most recently, Sky News! Become an expert in your field overnight (well in less than 12 weeks with Alexa) and watch yourself and your business hit new heights!

My last piece of advice is don't think about it, as Nike and Alexa say, 'JUST DO IT!'"

Tim Wareing - www.twsports.org

UEFA A Licence Coach and author of 'Toddler Soccer - The Essential Guide' and '1-on-1 Coaching - The Secrets To Improve ALL Football Players - GUARANTEED!'

"Anyone with a blog can claim to be an 'expert', but if you want to be an authority you need to write a book. If you've thought of writing one, but don't know where to start then this book is for you! It takes you by the hand and leads you through the step-by-step process - I should know, I've written one. Alexa's easy-to-read style and helpful hints will get you on your book writing journey in no time, and if you need any help along the way, she's there to help. I used Alexa and her team at The Book Refinery to write my book, and even if you've just got a few strands of ideas floating about in your head, Alexa will draw them out and help you get that book written. The process is remarkably straightforward and Alexa keeps you focused. I cannot recommend Alexa, or this book, highly enough."

Tony Messer - www.pickaweb.co.uk

Author of the Amazon 5-star rated 'The Lazy Website Syndrome'

"'Publish Your Way to More Clients' will help you produce and publish your book in far less time than it took me to write my first. The 7-step process really works, you just need to follow it.

If you spend time on each process and get them right, the writing will be super easy, because all you're doing is essentially filling in the gaps.

If you're going to write a book, there is no better person to work with than Alexa. She will help you through the process. If you can hire her and her team, then I would recommend you do so. I did and it made the process so much easier.

I spent almost two years writing my first book and most of that was spent in fear and procrastination (which will be your most ardent enemies). However with Alexa's help and endless encouragement, it got done – and I'm now embarking on my second.

Take action, get it done and the feeling you get when your book arrives is just... well, you'll know what I mean when yours arrives!

Remember - "If you have a book problem, if no one else can help, and if you can find them, maybe you can hire the A-Team" – Corny, I know, but it had to be done."

David Taylor - www.sheridonaccounting.com

Author of 'How to Get it Right and Grow Your Business with Confidence'

"If you want to grow your customer base and circle of influence, you're not alone. If you've heard that becoming an author is a great way to position yourself as an expert so customers find you rather you having to chase them, then I can assure you it's true...how do I know? Because a few years ago I was in exactly the same position as you are now.

Back then I didn't have the advantage of a book like this to guide me through the process, but luckily I did hear about Alexa and her ability to help aspiring authors get a book published. I contacted her and it proved to be the beginning of a great relationship, as she guided me through the creation and publication of three books.

As you've probably guessed from the fact I've written three, each book has repaid the effort and investment that went into publishing it many times over, with bookings for speaking engagements and actual buying customers.

Having read Alexa's book from cover to cover, I can tell you I wish she'd written it years ago because it contains pure gold for aspiring authors, by simplifying what can seem a complicated and sometimes overwhelming process into something that is easy to understand and follow.

I urge you to read it for yourself, then take a brave pill and get writing...I promise you won't regret it and remember, if you ever do get stuck you can always ask Alexa for help like I did!"

Simon Lotinga - www.simonlotingaconsulting.com

Author of 'The Seven Most Expensive Mistakes Salon Owners Make', 'The Salon Owner's Guide To Beating The Recession' and 'The Salon Owner's Bible'

"If you have ever thought you have a book inside you, but don't know how you're going to transfer your knowledge onto paper, then read this book first! Writing a book is not as hard as you may think. Alexa has created a very clear, step-by-step guide to becoming an author. If I can do it, you can too, with a little help from The Book Refinery."

Simon Banks - www.getvideoright.com

Author of 'How to Get Video Right'

"Thank you Alexa for writing this book. I know from my own experience, when I had an idea for a book, I kept putting it off because I didn't know where to start. It took me seven years to actually write my first book 'Awarded By Angels'. I hadn't found Alexa then, so I went via the publishing contract route.

I wasn't happy when I saw my royalties. I thought, 'why should they make money on my book?' It was my work! So, when I was able, I got out of their contract and self-published with Alexa. Then my second book was followed by my third and now my fourth: my first children's book.

If I had found 'Publish Your Way to More Clients' back then, it would have made my journey so much easier.

I love the comprehensive info and how it's broken down into steps. It's so valuable to a want-to-be author! There, I've said the A word. Come on, get your book in print and stake your place in the 'go to expert' realm.

Becoming an established author has added value and credibility to my work; my life's calling. I was able to hike my prices to their true worth!

Buy the book, then get Alexa as your book coach and experience the simple, seamless and totally natural way of working and getting your book into print."

Alison Ward (Angel Alison Ward) - www.www.alisonwardmentoring.com

Author of 'Bringing You back to You!', 'Awarded by Angels', 'Get That Friday Feeling' and the soon-to-be-published 'Where is the Pot of Gold?'

"Alexa's book is exactly the kick up the backside every entrepreneur needs if they are serious about growing their business.

Writing a book about your profession is the easiest way to elevate yourself to expert and leading authority, and this book will show you how.

Alexa shows you how to get started by defining your niche and telling you how to overcome the obstacles faced when writing a book. Chapter Four takes you through probably the most important aspect: mindset. Guiding you through the minefield of emotional barriers, she shows you exactly how to push past those difficult periods when most people either give up completely or stop indefinitely.

Throughout the book, there is lots of extra help in the form of directions to additional downloadable resources.

Having written a lead generation book myself, and being only too aware of the challenges that every budding author encounters, I would make life easy and avoid all the pain and discomfort by taking advantage of Alexa's expertise.

While writing my book, she was there every step of the way and helped me through the writing blocks, confusion and self-doubt that I'm sure everyone who writes a book will experience."

Mo Yusuff - www.clubrowcreations.co.uk

Author of 'Promo Power Supremacy'

Foreword

Well – of all the usages of time you and I could engage in – there's one towering head and shoulders (and heart and soul) above most of the life-wasting rest.

It's writing. Now; not just any writing – oh no! But an outpouring of your knowledge, your expertise, your experiences.

Why? Because it's every human's duty to help others on the path.

But there's more: just think of the increase in status, credibility, connections, earnings, income, and time coming from being a published author.

Did you know: published authors' fees for their 'other work' increase just as soon as their first book is published? (And yes, this includes self-published books too.)

My career as a consultant, speaker and subsequently information product creator and mentor started when I published my first book. Now 3 books later, 7 tips booklets, 100+ audio programs, 100+

programs – I'm still writing and recording.

What a fabulous way to help others –and be rightfully and justly rewarded for the positive differences made.

Now if you want to get your book out there, helping those fellow travellers on this spinning blue – you're in the right place, with the right person.

Alexa will be your experienced guide. Everyone needs one of those don't they?

How else will we climb mountains?

Enjoy the thrill!

Peter Thomson

"The UK's Most Prolific Information Product Creator"

Contents

Contents

Introduction

Expert (noun) – somebody skilled or knowledgeable. Somebody with a great deal of knowledge about, or skill, training, or experience in a particular field or activity
– Encarta Dictionary (U.K.)

Why You Need to be an Expert (in the eyes of your clients)

When searching for help, people, be it clients or customers, want to deal with experts. They want to feel safe and secure knowing that who they're dealing with really understands their issues, and trust that the person they are seeking knows how to fix them..

Being good in business isn't enough; you need to be perceived as an 'expert' to gain trust, which then axiomatically attracts new customers and clients effortlessly and easily.

In the world of the Internet, there are many, many avenues of tapping into information and resources. People who are looking for help are generally more educated and far more discerning with whom they trust and pay money to use. (Not to mention the copious amounts of free training and information that is now available on the internet.)

Anyone who is given the choice of dealing with either someone who is an expert (specialising in their area of need, being a published author in that particular subject, and other accreditations) or someone who is merely 'just another business owner/service provider', with no obvious signs of an in-depth understanding within that niche, is obviously going to chose the expert.

Experts educate. They can't wait to share their wisdom with the masses. They see themselves as a channel through which they contribute their gifts to the world.

In this book, I'm going to be sharing with you how you can declare your expertise in such a way that clients and customers will automatically seek you out. Marketing today is tough. There are so many new avenues to keep track of. Social media is on the rise at an alarming rate – and if you're not instagraming, facebooking, tweeting and snapchatting, not to mention all the other ways of conventional marketing, getting new, targeted clients into your sales funnel is exhausting. Finding a way to quickly demonstrate that you are the 'only logical choice' in the eyes of your potential clients, is crucial, and there is no better way than writing a book.

Now before I go any further, I'm also going to assume that you are in fact an expert already.

"I *am?*" I hear you say.

Yes, you are! This book isn't about what you need to learn within your industry, this book is about unlocking the 'expert' you *already are.*

I don't know how long you've been running your business for, perhaps you've just started, or you've been running it for 20+ years, but what I am going to assume is that you:

   ✓   Are passionate about what you do.

✓ Are knowledgeable to the extent that your clients reach their goals.

✓ Understand that 'educating' is key to helping them achieve that success.

✓ Are not afraid of 'giving away' your knowledge in the promotion of your business.

✓ Have a real desire to help your clients succeed.

✓ Have an in-depth understanding in one key area of your business.

If you identify with most of the above, then you're already an expert, you just need to let other people know it. Of course, telling people you're an expert isn't the solution. Being an expert is not something you can brand yourself, it's something that is 'attributed' to you by others, which is why it's critical to demonstrate your knowledge.

And the quickest easiest way of doing that is to write a book.

Now, I'm not talking about your memoir… unfortunately there may only be a handful of people who would be interested in that. No, I'm talking about a book that demonstrates your expertise, but at the same time, answers your clients most burning question, or shares the solution to their biggest headache.

This is where you specialise (niche) your thinking; where you become the expert within your business sector. If you can demonstrate your knowledge and then write a book that explains how to fix the problem – then your book will be the best lead attraction tool in your toolbox.

Not sure if you have that type of information to hand? Don't panic! This is exactly why I've written this book, to show you how to brainstorm ideas and get your book published quickly and easily.

So, to quickly summarise, here is what you need to understand before we go any further:

- Experts are deemed 'the only logical choice' in the eyes of potential clients.

- Specialising within your business is key, as you can then talk to a specific group of people and demonstrate your knowledge much more effectively.

- Writing a book is one of the most powerful ways of demonstrating your expertise.

Right let's get cracking… and move onto the first part of the book, 'how to reveal your inner expert' – it's easier than you think.

An assumption

Marketing has come a long way in the past few years. When I wrote the first version of this book, lead pages and email marketing were critical – whereas now, having a strong social media presence is equally important.

I'm surprised at how websites are being designed. They seem to be relying heavily on the visual aspect, rather than content – and I'm really curious as to how well those websites are converting. (Although in my view, you can have both, a stunningly beautiful website, as well as lots of information. How frustrated do you get with websites that hide their info details? It drives me potty – and I wonder at the tactic of not having these details easily accessible?)

I'm still of the belief that educating your customers is a critical part of your marketing, and by writing your book, it will become the front and centre of your marketing campaign. If you're unfamiliar with a lead generator (or lead magnet as it's sometimes called) then very quickly, it's something you give away for free, or for very little money, to get the customer's name and contact details, enabling you to market to them. This book is all about becoming an author for this purpose. You are going to use your book as a lead generator – to get people into your marketing funnel.

Chapter 1

How to Reveal Your 'Inner Expert'

"'Expert' is something others call you, and something you demonstrate, not a title you claim yourself."

The traditional path to becoming an expert is to spend a lifetime in the industry earning relevant educational certifications and degrees. But this method takes a long time, and is impractical for the new entrepreneur who wants to hit the road running. It also doesn't *just* take education to be an expert, it takes hands-on experience with a level of success within that field.

Of course, having accreditations is essential in some areas of business, like coaching and training, accountancy or law, etc. but having to study for years and years is not necessarily the only option open to you. As long as you are genuinely learning the best methods to help your potential clients solve their problems, (and they are achieving the results) then I can safely assume that you are in fact already an expert, it's just a case of unleashing that knowledge and channelling it in a condensed and targeted way, so that you can start letting them see that for themselves.

Yes, it takes extra effort and extra work, but that's what differentiates you from all the other business owners out there. Most people aren't willing to put in the time and commitment, they just want to get rich quick, and try to sell to as many people as possible. And I personally hate that type of marketing.

To be an expert takes extra effort and extra work, what most people aren't willing to put in. That's why it's a bell curve. That's why high performers perform in the far right side because they will spend the time and the energy that it takes to be involved here as an expert. ~ **Bryan Neale**

Let's go back to the definitions of what I believe are associated with being an expert.

An expert:

- ✓ Is passionate about what he/she does
- ✓ Has an in-depth understanding in one key area of their business.
- ✓ Has a real desire to help his/her clients succeed.
- ✓ Is knowledgeable to the extent that his/her clients reach their goals
- ✓ Is not afraid of 'giving away' his/her knowledge in the promotion of his/her business
- ✓ Understands that 'educating' is key to helping him/her achieve that success.

Let's look at some of these qualities, and see how you can start demonstrating them to your audience.

Be Passionate About What you do

This is *essential* in my eyes. If you're not passionate about what you do, then why do it? If you think it's going to make money then it might to begin with, but your overall satisfaction and level of success will diminish over time.

However, I'm not going to argue with those that have become rich and successful with 'get rich quick schemes'. We all know there are people out there that have achieved that. I'm interested in talking to people who have a true desire to help others and are passionate about the results that their clients achieve.

So, I'm going to assume that: you're someone who is running a business; that you are *passionate about it*, and that you *really want your clients to achieve success*.

Find Your Area of Specialism (Niche)

"Many differentiate themselves by looking at their competition and finding a niche. It's important to remember to start with you first. Define what is unique and special about you, then analyse your competitors to see if what you're offering is viable and/or how to communicate it in a unique way. Otherwise you define yourself via others and sell out from the very beginning."
~ Josef Shapiro, Director of E-Myth Academy

One of the key factors in becoming an expert is knowing something intimately and there is one quick way to achieve this; niching. Finding a specific area within your business sector then becoming an 'expert' within it. This is critical because it differentiates you from all the 'other service providers' who are generalists, rather than specialists.

Being a business that caters for 'everyone' is almost impossible. You have to communicate to a very large community of people in generalities, rather than to a specific audience.

Think about your business for a minute.

→ Does your business try and cater to 'everyone'?

→ Do you find yourself being compared on price, and not the service you offer?

→ Are you struggling to keep up with the changing market?

If you answered yes to these questions, then it might be worth considering a rethink in your business plan. Being all things to all people is really hard work, not to mention expensive.

Trying to catch all the fish in the sea is time consuming and costs a lot of money, as you have to trawl large areas of ocean, and you never know what you're going to catch. But if you decided to catch 'Alaskan Snow crab' you could find out where they breed, what the best bait is, and become practised in crabbing. You then market your crab as a speciality item and charge a premium for it. It's a simplified analogy, but I hope you can see the point I'm trying to make. Being a generalist also limits your opportunity to charge a premium price.

Take five minutes to think of which area in your business you have most resonance with. Write it down, and make some notes. What draws you to that area? Do you have a specific qualification that makes you an ideal professor of this niche? Do some research and check out any possible competition. How could you differentiate yourself? What could make you a leader in this field?

Once you've established your area of interest, and done your competition research, think about how you can now drill into that area and carve yourself an area to become a specialist in.

I would imagine that you're naturally drawn to a part of your current business that you have some special affinity with. Perhaps you studied it at school, or you've found that a good majority of your clients need help with this area. When you're comfortable with your decision (and don't underestimate this process) then you can start to tailor your business to accommodate that group of clients.

If you're completely stuck (and have already done the exercise above) then write down your current USP (Unique Selling Proposition). What is it, at this point in time, that you stand for? For instance, if you're a fitness instructor, what does that encompass? Do you offer fitness advice for everyone, or is it specifically for women, or men? If it's both, which would you prefer to focus on? Do you teach all areas of fitness, or do you like the nutrition part more than the exercise part? Do you specialise in weight training over cardio? If you currently do both, and are sticking to your core beliefs, could you specialise in just one area?

'Army style' boot camps are proving to be very popular, and a fantastic example of niching. They specialise in a 'specific style' of fitness, and appeal to an exclusive group of people, mostly men and women between the ages of 20 – 35, and I would assume to more men than women. Taking a look at this example, could you create an 'army style' boot camp that was specifically for this group of people? Maybe you would like to niche further and provide this type of training targeted at women between the ages of 20 – 35. This then gives you a platform to tailor-make the course designed specifically for women, aged between 20 and 35, looking for a serious competitive fitness experience.

I hope I'm giving you some ideas on how you can specialise? Could you use the example I have given and see if there is something you can adopt into your practice?

Let's look at another example. Perhaps you are an accountant and your business model is to provide accounting for any business owner. Your marketing will have to cater to everyone, and no one specific. You will be 'just another accountant' shouting out 'use me' in an ocean saturated with them. So, what can you do that will make you stand out? Do you have to be the cheapest accountant to grab someone's attention? No, not great for business and you'll be doing yourself a massive disservice if you're just trying to price cut everyone else! Don't be price driven to be noticed, be a specialist in accountancy and charge a premium price for it. You could niche into one sector, focus your attention on a specific area, like tax specialists for companies who turn over 1 million a year and then concentrate on learning all the strategies needed for this area of accountancy. Then, when you have your target market established (large companies with 20+ employees and a turnover of 1 million) you advertise to those specific companies. You can charge a premium price, as you are the 'go to person' who caters specifically for their needs, and knows all the tricks and techniques for lowering their tax bill.

If the thought of niching is causing you to come out in a cold sweat, why don't you try it out first. So, taking the accounting example above – have a look at your most common clients and see if they are a particular group of people. Perhaps you have lots of self-employed clients, and on average they turn over 25k a year. Could you start some messaging like, 'Succeed Accountancy' – specialising in Self-employed tax. Just that one small strap line will demonstrate that you deal specifically with that type of accountancy – and over time, self-employed business owners could then be the only people you work with.

Of course, it's important you choose your niche carefully – you don't want to be working with people who you're not genuinely interested in, but I hope the above example gives you some idea on how to get this niching established. (And I don't advocate you do this overnight!)

Become an Expert by Learning all you can

Once you've identified your area of speciality then the next step is to learn all you can about that particular area. Now some of you might already have this box ticked, which is fantastic – now it's all about focusing on those people.

Read up on the latest research (if that's appropriate) or techniques used. If you're unfamiliar with them, then get familiar with them.

✓ **Join forums**, participate in discussions, and see what people in this area are talking about and needing assistance with. LinkedIn has some great focus groups, and the discussions on there are insightful and a fantastic resource for new information. **Facebook** is also proving a fantastic platform for finding out valuable insights. See top tip on next page.

✓ **Keep up-to-date with the latest publications** on the subject as well. This will also help you with the later strategy of writing a book, as you will be familiar with the latest titles, know which ones to use, and which ones to avoid.

✓ **Keep up-to-date with news and trends as well.** It's smart to keep ahead of the pack, and if you can keep ahead of the trends and then be able offer these, (e.g. latest apps, which social media platform to use and latest business practices) to your clients, you will be successful and popular.

Don't be Afraid of 'Giving Away' your Knowledge in the Promotion of Your Business

Hopefully, we've now established your niche, (or at least given you some ideas as to how to identify an area on which to focus) the next step is to *educate* your audience and not be afraid to share your knowledge, and give away information at the front end, to educate and inform potential clients.

You must let your potential clients know that you understand their needs and that you can solve them.

Educating your potential clients is a great way of setting you up as an expert, as you will be establishing your credibility. There are a lot of people that I trust inherently on many subjects, simply because they're not shy to share their knowledge, and they're not trying to sell me anything. They just want to be helpful in their own area of expertise. These are not just people that I learn from, but also people that I would buy from because they've demonstrated their credibility.

If I was given a choice between two new fitness coaches: Coach one just wanted to sell me their course, with nothing more than a price list and their times of availability, and Coach two, who had a questionnaire designed about the specific goals I wanted to achieve; information on some useful stretches and how that will help my training, and some more information on how the course was designed, using the latest techniques, which coach am I more likely to trust, and therefore use? Probably coach two. They weren't trying to sell me anything, they just wanted to educate me first, and make sure I understood how the course was going to benefit me. Big difference!

So, don't be afraid to give away some of your knowledge, up front and for nothing. Make it relevant, and specific.

 Top Tip: One of the most popular ways of doing this is to start a facebook or a LinkedIn group. I'm a member of several groups on Facebook, and the knowledge that they impart is fantastic. They also draw in like-minded people – who are also willing to share their information and you might find this a great place to soundboard your ideas.

No doubt you've got lots of information about your area of interest. Spend five minutes thinking about how you can use that information (or edit it so that it fits in with your newly identified niche.) If you're in the service industry, perhaps you could write a leaflet or booklet that you can use straight away about your specific methodology or approach. Quote some history or unknown facts about this method. Use your imagination and don't be boring. Make it all about your client, not about how long you've been studying and why it interests you.

Now Tell the World About it, Write a Book!

So now that you've unleashed your inner expert - having specialised knowledge within an area of speciality - understanding the importance of sharing your gift, the next step is get the ultimate calling card: a book. Like I've said before, nothing says 'expert' more than being an author. It's one of the greatest accolades you can have.

As one of my past clients said in his testimonial:

> *In terms of what becoming an author has done for me, well it's really made me an expert in my field. It has propelled me higher than anything I have ever done, and since publishing the book in Feb of 2010 – it's been sold in over 18 different countries. It puts you in the forefront of your industry and it's opened up interviews on the BBC radio, and led to newspaper articles. So in terms of my whole business, it's just really strengthened who I am, and what I stand for.*
> *- Tim Wareing, author of 'Toddler Soccer'*

Update 2017: Tim has gone to write two more books - '1 on 1 Coaching' and 'The Secrets to Developing ELITE Youth Football Players.' which have been sold in over 20 countries. Becoming an author has revolutionised his marketing strategy and he's even been given PR opportunities from the likes of Sky News.

Despite the prevalence of the Internet, and the ubiquitous e-books that are out there, print publications still carry a lot of weight, because it takes more steps to be a published author of a properly printed publication than an online one, and doing so can really boost your credibility.

The next part of this book is all about how you can write one. Hopefully I've helped you establish what you're good at so the next steps should be relatively simple, Writing a book might seem daunting but with the right guidance and planning, you too can be a published author within twelve weeks.

 If you have an idea for a book, or you've already got material written and not sure what to do with it next, then why not get in touch. Simply email me alexa@thebookrefinery.com, and we can look at what steps to take next.

How to use Your Book – a Quick Overview

Now that we've established what a book can do (a platform for showing off your inner expertness) I'm quickly going to go over how you use it in your marketing plan. Simply put, this book will be offered at the front end of your marketing strategy. You're going to use it as your lead generator – either by giving it away free – or offering it at the front end for an irresistible price. What price you charge needs to be *tested.* I've had clients try various options; giving it away 'free' (but charging posting and Packing) and selling for both a full and a discounted price. Results are varied. But remember, your main aim is to get readers to buy your higher priced back end services - and I go into much more detail throughout the book.

However, before we start with the how to – there are a few bits of research we need to do first and I explain what those are in the three critical questions in the next chapter.

Once we've done that, the next six chapters are all about how to write a book for this purpose. My area of expertise is helping business owners write books purely for lead generation (not how to be a best seller, although if that happens naturally then great stuff!). Self-publishing is extremely popular, as it allows you the control of what you write and how you sell and distribute it. Writing with the specific purpose of getting on a 'best seller' list, or making money from the front-end sales, is incredibly difficult and almost impossible. I don't want to sound defeatist or negative, but the number of people who try to get their book endorsed by a large publishing house is staggering, and in fact, rather depressing. The statistics are (at the time of writing) that less than 0.1% of authors become best sellers, and it's a very hard statistic to argue with.

Self-publishing allows you the freedom to use your own marketing strategy to target your specific audience. You can then set up special lead pages that offer your book, and direct traffic to those lead pages, with print advertisements and other marketing tactics (I go into much more detail about how to do this in Chapter 7).

You can also sell your book on sites like Amazon.com, as well as other large Internet based book selling companies, by directing customers or clients to buy your book from there.

Summary

So in this chapter we have looked at the two key strategies unlocking your inner expert:

- ✓ Being a specialist on one specific area

- ✓ Becoming a published author (publishing a book that talks about that niche).

We've looked at how you can start narrowing down your area of focus, as well as looking at ways in which to educate your potential clients, and not being afraid of giving away information at the front end, which in turn engages trust, and sets you apart from all the other business owners who are just trying to sell their services.

Having a published book in your marketing literature is the ultimate business card, as you service two objectives in one hit; educating your potential customer, and setting yourself up as an 'expert'.

Now let's move on and look at how easy it is to write a book in less than 12 weeks.

Chapter 2

Debunking the Myth of how Hard it is to Write a Book

Nothing brings you expert status faster than being the author of a book.

Nothing positions you more than a book

Without doubt, writing a book and getting it published propels the reader's perception that you really know what you're talking about. It reinforces the reader's belief, that if you can write over 64 pages, and get it into print, then you must have a passion and in-depth knowledge of the subject you have written about.

It's one of those magical things; as soon as someone sees your name in print your 'expert' status automatically jumps up several notches.

Writing a book increases your credibility and enhances all aspects of your marketing strategies, from networking, to public speaking. This is not a secret, it's simply a tactic that most people are unsure of how to implement.

Somehow publishing is seen as a complicated process, when all it means is writing, printing and distribution. That's it!

So having established that becoming an author will make you stand out from the crowd, what about the writing process?

"Surely I need to write well to publish a book?"

That can be answered with a 'yes' and 'no'.

Yes, it's important to be able to write a coherent sentence. No one is going to read a book that is either badly written, or doesn't make any sense. BUT you don't have to be Shakespeare to write a book.

In fact, with proper planning (which I go into detail later) and using the '7-Step Process', you will be able to write a book quickly and easily, with no need for in-depth qualifications in English literature.

One of the first rules of writing a book for lead generation is that it's of interest to your readers (or target audience). For example, if you write a book called, 'My Life As An Accountant' there might only be a handful of people interested enough to buy and read it. (Remember the memoir example I mentioned in the intro?)

Therefore, you need to make sure your book is all about your clients or specific audience. We've already looked at niching your business, now it's time to focus on that niche and get to the purpose of your book. I talk about this more in Chapter Three, but for now, why not think about what areas your clients have the most problem with. What is the most popular question you're asked? How can you use that information within your book?

You don't need to be Shakespeare to write a book.

It's true! As I said, you don't have to have any qualifications in writing, or be able to come up with verse like Shakespeare to be a published author. You just need to be engaging and able to impart information that your target audience (and I'll be explaining who your target audience is later, it's critical to know this) wants to learn, and read about.

There are also different ways that you can get your book written. You can type it, hand write it and then get someone to type it up, or simply record your book by speaking into a recording device, and get it transcribed.

Whatever way you choose, just remember to get it professionally proof-read, (and in some cases copy-edited) so that it's comprehensible and engaging enough to inspire your audience to learn more. Getting that right is key, and I explain this strategy in much more detail in the next chapter.

If you're still unsure of how easy it is…or where to start, my next point will explain why it's easier than you think.

With Proper Planning, it Really is Simple

Over the years I have discovered a strategy that is really useful and in fact critical, for getting your thoughts and ideas down into a coherent format and useable.

Using a system which I call the *'Blueprint Plan'*, it makes this process easy and logical, and captures all your ideas in one place, so that writing your book flows effortlessly and quickly.

I teach it to all my clients, and they have found it to be an essential component in their publishing projects. The great news is that this system is devised using free software, which can be easily installed on your computer. Or you can use pen and paper (it's still my favourite method).

I will also be explaining the components you need within your book, to produce a great publication.

Don't dismiss writing a book as too difficult or time consuming, it will be one of the best marketing and positioning tools you can have in your business. I really hope this book helps you get your writing project finished and published, and most importantly of all, into the hands of your future big-paying clients.

The Kudos of being an 'Amazon' Five Star Rated Author

My mentor and colleague Ed Rivis has written three books and all of them have achieved either a five or 4.5 star rating on Amazon. This hasn't happened overnight. The material he publishes is of high quality, and he is also an expert in what he writes about, so it's of little surprise that he's been awarded such a high rating.

And it hasn't been that difficult.

His first book took him a while to finish, but that was down to not having a firm plan in place, and the book kept getting pushed down on the 'to do' list. However, as soon as he reinstated some accountability and got a book coach on board, it got finished and out into the world, relatively quickly.

And almost like children, the second wasn't long to follow. 'Email Marketing Dynamite' was produced within 2 months, and was preceded by '*Massive Traffic*' which took just one week to produce. Once you've written your first book, the others seem to flow instinctively, as the seemingly complicated process is de-mythed and structures are in place to makes it easier.

As Ed says himself…

"I know it sounds like a cliché, but becoming an author has changed my life.

In 2003 I was just another 'web developer' churning out websites for whatever clients were willing to pay. They were forcing me to compete on price with other web design agencies in my local region of North Yorkshire and it was tough winning jobs.

However once my book appeared on Amazon, all of a sudden I found that people were coming to me, rather than the other way round. They were asking if I would kindly develop them a website, and although I won't say they had an open chequebook, I would certainly say it changed the way they spoke to me. They understood, just by the simple fact that I had a book – a 5 star rated book on Amazon - that I was an expert and they presumed my pricing would reflect that fact.

Once my first book was written (incidentally I used a book coach to help me, as my first draft kept being left 'on the shelf') and with her help, it became a well thought out book, containing great advice and help – and once it got into the hands of prospects – reviews were naturally left on Amazon. You can of course go one step further, and ask for your readers to leave reviews, but you should do so carefully. Don't ask for 'good' reviews – ask for their honest opinion, and secondly, if you are going to ask a group of people, then stagger the requests.

One issue I had with my second book – Email Marketing Dynamite – one person didn't believe the reviews that were left about that book (there were about 30 or so, all in a space of a few days) instead he thought I had written them, which obviously wasn't true. So do be careful in your strategy of obtaining reviews for your book.

Having a 5 star rating on my book, does indeed compel people's belief that I am an expert. If you can at least say you are an Amazon 4 star rated author, or Amazon 5 star rated author, that's obviously going to give you kudos in the minds of your targeted audience."

You can hopefully see now why this accolade could really help you achieve the kudos associated with being available on sites like Amazon.

The 3 Critical Questions you Need to Ask Before you Start

Before you start planning or writing your book, you need to ask yourself three simple questions.

If you don't, then your book might not do what you want it to, and your writing effort could result in little or no response and be a total waste of money and time. So, please don't skip this step.

Don't be afraid to go out into the market place and find out the answers, you'll be in a much better position if you do, as you'll be starting the project with a knowledge that your book is wanted, will be read, and be confident that it generates the desired response you want (targeted enquiries for your back-end services).

The 3 Critical Questions:

1. Do you have a **clear message** to write about?

2. Do people want to **know what it is you're writing about?**

3. What is your **desired response** once people have read your book?

1. Do you have a clear message to write about?

What is the message you want people to know? What do you want people to use your service for? Are you the person who can provide the solution? If your answer is, "well I stand for a lot of things", then you need to distil your message into one clear distinct area.

Remember how I explained establishing your niche in the previous chapter? This is where it comes into play.

This book you're reading isn't about business strategy, it's about how to identify your expertise and write a book that cements that status.

The books that work best are the ones that are niched, books that offer a solution to one particular challenge, and it's your job as an author to be clear in what that challenge is.

What is the core message or question you want to answer in your publication? What is going to make people buy or request your book? What is your angle or hook?

2. Do people want to know what it is you're writing about?

I mentioned before about being niched, but remember, you need to be niched in an area of interest.

This is why it's critical to stand for something, and the more distinct that something is, the easier it is to explain. But does that then lend to writing a book about it?

If the answer is an obvious 'YES' (and you can hop over to www.amazon.co.uk to see what other books are out there already) then this can give you a great indication of the need for the subject.

If the answer is 'not sure', then why not ask your target audience? Or if you're still finding your niche, try one of the following:

→ Run a survey with your current list of clients that you want to niche into.

→ Ask these clients what their most burning questions/biggest challenges are.

→ Read relevant publications and see what the common issue/problem is.

→ Join forums on places like LinkedIn and facebook and listen to what people are having issues with.

Whatever you choose, do your research.

Finding out what the audience wants to read is the first step to producing a highly desirable publication. It may seem obvious, but many don't do this research.

3. What is your 'call to action'/desired response?

Writing your book to gain repute is of course one of the main results of becoming a published author. However, there is also one more essential ingredient your book must contain in order for it to be a successful and profitable lead generator.

This ingredient is: Your 'Call to Action'.

It's all very well writing over sixty-four pages highlighting a problem, and how you are the 'go to' person to fix it but if you don't give a strong, easy to follow 'call to action' (what you want the person to do, once they have read the book) then the readers won't take action.

Don't assume that just because you've outlined the solution to the readers' biggest challenge, they will then pick up the phone, or get in touch. **You have to tell them**, and you'll need to do this more than once.

 Take five minutes to think about what you want the readers to do once they read the book. Do you want them to;

→ Call you?

→ Visit your website?

→ Visit a specific website, like a lead page?

→ Get into a sales funnel... if so, how?

→ Buy another product/service that you offer?

→ Use another 'call to action'?

If you're not clear on this, then you will be leaving potential clients on the table.

Have a think about your 'call to action'. This can be any number of things, depending on the complexity of your services, but make it clear and state it several times.

You can also have several other smaller calls to action throughout your book offering further information (by visiting your main website) or free downloads that your readers will find valuable, but don't offer too many. Give the readers too many choices and they won't take any action at all!

Summary

In this chapter we've looked at the two main reasons why you should write a book, and the three critical questions you should ask before you start.

Once you have written and published your book, you have a platform to grow your business; you've established yourself as the 'expert' and the 'go to' person within your industry, and everyone who receives and reads your book is then a potential future customer.

Don't forget to ask the three questions: Is it a clear message? Have you established the need to share this information? And most importantly of all, what do you want the reader to do once they have read it?

When you get your 'call to action' established, this then opens up new revenue opportunities, like additional information products, services, and speaking opportunities which will then bring in new leads and sales on your back end.

Getting a book coach is one of the easiest solutions to this challenge, as they can help answer the questions outlined, and make sure the 'call to action' is clear and easy. Simply visit www.thebookrefinery.com and head to Our Services Section of the website. Let's see how I can help you get that book out of your head and into print.

With the right tools and support, writing a book can be quick and painless, and the benefits of being an 'author' outshine the effort required to be one. With the right help, you too can publish your way to more clients.

Chapter 3

The Importance of Planning

*"Before everything else,
getting ready is the secret of success."*
- Henry Ford

My experience of working with business owners who want to become published authors is: they have a ton of knowledge, and are really passionate about what they do, but they don't have a clear idea of what to write about, who their target audience is, and what the 'call to action' should be.

All of these can be solved with proper planning. In this chapter I will be explaining why you need to be clear on **what** you are writing about (which includes doing some research first) and then making sure your book is well planned first *before you start* typing or recording.

Get this part right before you begin, and you will produce a cohesive, easy to read book, which will convert readers into high paying customers or clients. Skip on this step, and you will find it difficult to keep going, and the writing will be a struggle.

What to Write About

What your book needs to highlight is the problem your target audience is facing, and why they need to know the solution. You then offer the solution in the 'call to action' (more about what the 'call to action' is later in this chapter).

Therefore, you need to establish your target's *biggest challenge*. What is it that they want to know the answers to? What is it that they struggle to achieve, or get help with? Once you identify that, you can then write about it and offer a solution.

If you are unsure about what that is, go back to *'Chapter 2, The Three Critical Questions'* – what is the core message you're writing about?

If you are writing a 'How to' book, then you need to be careful NOT to give away all the answers. Yes, you want to give enough away that it whets their appetite for more, but not so much that they don't need your services for help. Remember – your call to action is to get them spending more money with you. It's to lead them into your sales funnel, be it a higher priced product (training) or one on one services.

> The goal of the book is to get targeted clients into your marketing funnel, so that they then buy your high priced back end items.

Is your book wanted?

Okay, so you've established that your customer's most frustrating problem is X (using one of the methods suggested in *'Chapter 2 – ask the audience'* etc.). The next question is, is that enough of a problem/challenge to write a book about it? I'm more than confident it is.

Don't however just start writing a book without this type of *planning first*. I had a potential client call me up recently looking for help to self-promote a book she was planning on writing. After a few initial questions it became clear that she had no idea if her book was even wanted. She had no target audience to ask, and it was on an extremely niched subject (in fact, so niched there were no similar titles on Amazon, which is quite telling in itself) but also, the information on the subject she was writing about was abundant on the Internet, and all for free!

She also had no client list to speak of (so she hadn't asked her audience) and it wasn't her core business either (it was a parallel one). My advice to her was to stop what she was doing, write a small free report (from the pages she had written already) and make that available for free on her website, and then see how many people requested it. The result from that test would then decide if the need for an entire book was required.

Don't assume that because you are writing a book, people will automatically want to read it; do your research first, find out your target audience's biggest challenge, and see if there are other books out there that cover that topic.

Once you've identified a need for your information, you can explain the challenge and why your target audience needs to know the solution, then use the 'call to action' (within the book) to help them get the answer.

You know more than you think

When you sit down and start to think about what it is you're solving, you'll probably find your pen won't stop. Most of my clients are surprised at how easy it is to come up with ideas of what to write about once they've identified their specialised area.

Don't be worried that you don't 'know enough'. Once you get your plan started you will probably find that you will have more than enough information, and actually have to prune down your ideas. I had one client who realised he had enough ideas for three separate books; he's writing his second one now!

You are the expert on what you are writing about, so trust that knowledge, and get all of your ideas down on paper. You can then use these when you start planning your book. You might even find you have more than one book in you.

Establishing Who Your Target Audience is

Once you've got your core message, your target audience should then become apparent. (You might already have a clear target audience, which is great.)

Hopefully, your customer list consists of those specific people we identified earlier, but sometimes if you have a large list, it might become clear that a percentage of them are not your target audience at all. (Don't worry about them, you'll probably find that a large percentage of those clients weren't using your services anyway.) What better time to write a book that identifies that and works for you to either prune your list down to fit your target audience, or lets you acquire new clients and customers that now fit in with your niche.

It's all about them, not YOU!

When you have identified who it is you're writing for, then it's very important that you write *to* them and not *at* them.

You are the expert, and it's very easy to forget that the people whom you are talking to need to be educated and spoken to in a way that is not full of 'tech speak', or full of words and phrases that only people in the industry know.

A fantastic example of this is when I helped Ed Rivis write his first book '*The Ultimate Web Marketing Strategy*', which was aimed at business owners. This is what we soon discovered (taken from an interview I did with Ed).

Ed: *"It was amazing how many assumptions I had made on the audience in terms of knowledge, of what I assumed they would already know about the topic I was writing about. As we discovered, as we worked through the book, we had to re-write vast chunks, where I had gone completely into geek speak, using terminology that only myself (or expert web designers/developers) would understand, but that wasn't who this book was aimed at. The book was aimed at the general everyday business owner (who probably didn't understand very technical web terms, in fact very likely would not understand complicated web site terminology). So working together with Alexa (for about 3 months) we went through it paragraph by paragraph, and took the language back into normal everyday words and phrases that I knew they would understand."*

So always remember who you are talking to and speak in their language.

Also, talk all about THEM, not you. See the challenges from their perspective and keep the terminology simple. Don't make the book about you – yes you need to convey that you can help people, but do it in a way it's all about the reader and not a soap box that's all about you and how fantastic you are. All you'll end up doing is putting the reader off, and they won't finish the book, let alone follow the 'call to action'!

> *"One hates an author that's all author."*
> **- George Gordon, Lord Byron, "Beppo"**

Your 'Call to Action'

This is one of the most important aspects of your book and the one that should be established BEFORE you start your writing. Having your 'call to action' firmly thought out first will get people responding once they've finished reading.

I encourage my clients to print it out, and stick it on their computer screen so that they constantly see it as they're writing. This way the 'call to action' is clear and inserted into the project seamlessly. You don't want your call to actions to come across as being salesy – or make it obvious you're trying to upsell. You want them to seem as an obvious next step – and it's something I talk about later on in the book (remember, you're not imparting how to turn lead into gold; it's about identifying the problem, agitating it and then providing the solution in the call to action.)

The 'call to action' should be the one response you want readers to do once they have finished reading your book.

Here are some examples:

→ Call for a no obligation consultation (with the aim of converting them to private coaching/training work).

→ Go to a specific web page, perhaps for more information, or a landing page, which up-sells them to another product.

→ Visit a particular website, and do something specific, like fill out an enquiry form.

How many should you have?

You can have more than one 'call to action', but I wouldn't have too many, or you'll find that your readers won't do anything.

So you can have a few smaller ones that invite the reader to visit particular web pages, where they can get free downloads that are specific to the topic you are writing about. Or for them to sign up to your blog, just remember to keep it simple and don't have too many.

Getting them right

 Identifying what you want your reader to do is crucial and if you're struggling with this you might find hiring a book coach useful. This is where the knowledge of someone who has helped coaching and training professionals write books for lead generation really pays off. I also have a cheat sheet that shows you how to write them on my website. Hop over to www.thebookrefinery.com/call-to-actions-cheat-sheet/ and click on the green 'Call to Actions Cheat Sheet' hyperlink.

Having an experienced writing coach who knows the subtleties of writing a strong and compelling 'call to action' will guarantee the book's ability to convert readers into clients.

How to Plan your Book

So, we've identified what to write about, the subject is in demand and you have a clear target audience in mind. You've also established exactly what you want your reader to do. Now for the exciting stuff!

Planning your book is essential. Without this step your book will take much longer to write, and be much more difficult, as you won't have a clear map of what it is going to say. All of this can be overcome quickly and easily by using a simple technique I mentioned in the last chapter; the 'Blueprint Plan'. I have to say, this is probably my favourite part of the process, as we get to see the book in its entirety – and when we've finished the session, my clients are always surprised with the results, if not really excited to get going.

The number one reason why books get abandoned is that this step has either not been done at all, or has only been done briefly. **Even though I emphasise this point, clients who don't follow this step always struggle.** I really understand the excitement of starting a project and wanting to jump in. You might have a working title, and have a really clear image of your book cover, but when it comes to content, it's really important to have a solid plan. You wouldn't dream of building a house without a proper plan, a detailed blueprint of what the house will look like once it's finished, how big it will be, what each room is used for, how many floors it will have etc.

The same should apply to a book.

Trust me, *I've seen what happens when people don't.*

Without this level of detail, you will struggle to write quickly and easily, as you won't know where you're starting from, or whether you'll be covering everything you need to. Also, as you will probably be writing this book over a period of time (and you may have a break or get busy and have to delay your writing). If you don't have a plan to fall back on, or remind you of the topics you want to cover, it'll prove tough to keep going. Lack of clarity is one of the main reasons we don't complete a project. I'm guilty of this, especially when it comes to starting a project – if I'm unclear of what I need to do, then I'll procrastinate starting.

I had one client who didn't start out with a plan, and when we looked at what he had written, he had gone off on a completely different tangent halfway through, which had nothing to do with the core message he was trying to convey. We fixed that quickly by re-grouping and produced a plan that got him back on track, and he completed his book within a few weeks.

Getting the right foundations in place and coming up with a 'Blueprint Plan', at the beginning - listing all the chapters, subheadings and notes - will make the writing process quick and easy.

There are a few ways you can produce this plan, but my three favourites are:

✓ Good old fashioned **pen and paper**

✓ **Mind-mapping** software

✓ **Notepad**, or any other non-formatting text editor. Non-formatting at the planning stage is essential and I will explain why later.

1. Pen and Paper

I use an A4 sheet of paper, which I turn to landscape orientation and put the title of the book in the middle. I then write the target audience in the left hand corner, along with the key call to action. I then have chapters coming off from the middle – much like I've shown below when using the mind mapping software.

This then gives you a complete overview of the book, in one glance.

2. Mind-mapping software

This is pretty much the same as above, just on your computer, plus it gives you the flexibility to add bits and to move things around. You can also export this to a word document, ready for you to type in the missing info.

There are numerous software packages out there, from expensive, high performing ones like Mindjet, available from www.mindjet.com; to free Shareware programs like Free Mind which is what I use. This is available from www.freemind.sourceforge.net.

Whichever one you choose, it's worth getting used to how it works, then you'll be able to get your ideas down instantly and easily. Most software comes with adequate training or some sort of 'Help' section, and you can usually find further tutorials online.

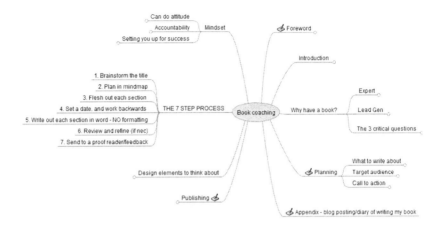

Figure 1 - Mindmap plan of book

Here is a snapshot of my mind map. This is the blueprint of the book you're reading. You can see how I've planned out each section, and what each chapter is going to cover. I can then add to each node building up a comprehensive and coherent plan, which I can expand on, either in Microsoft Word or a similar program.

Alternatively, if you're good at talking through your mind map you can orally record your book get it transcribed and edited and then you're good to go!

 For more information about this, check out my blog at www.thebookrefinery.com/writing/talk-your-book-instead/, which gives you all the information you need to know about recording your book.

---

3. Notepad

If mind-mapping software is not for you, or you're more comfortable with Notepad, then you can use this to plan out your book instead. It's worth noting that at this stage, it's a really good idea not to get caught up with any fancy formatting issues. It can be very distracting and time consuming. Getting carried away with making your plan look pretty, with font selection and other formatting features is a waste of time at this stage and I wouldn't recommend it. Also, don't use headers or footers – it's just distracting and a bit of a headache when you come to formatting your book ready for print. (I go into much more detail about formatting your book later.)

Here is a sample of a Notepad plan that I used when I first had an idea for my book. As you can see, it's based upon the same principles as the other methods I mention: chapter titles, headings, and then subheadings, all of which you can then just add to or move around.

```
File   Edit   Format   View   Help

Introduction
        Why you are writing this book

How to Use this book
        How to get the best out of this book
        Where to start
        Clear instructions on how to 'read' it

Chapter 1: Title of Chapter
        Intro about what about what the chapter is going to
        be covering
                Sub heading 1: The first Sub heading
                Why this is important
                How this can help
                        Heading 3:Another smaller category
                        write about that here
                        How it can help

                Sub heading 2: The second heading
                Why this is important
                How this can help
                Why you need it
```

Figure 2 - Notepad example of my book plan.

Whichever way you choose to create your plan, make sure that everything you need is included within it. If you create this on a computer, you can then add points, or change the order of chapters, but it's really critical to plan it first. I can't emphasise this point strongly enough (it's why I've repeated myself so much). Take the time to plan your book and make sure you're happy with it before you start writing.

What software you decide to use is really up to you. What is important is to get this plan done in as much detail as possible. I recommend you spend at least a week to 10 days getting this right (even longer in some cases) and refine and review, until you get to a point where you can just start typing your ideas, expanding the sections that you've outlined.

Remember: have a clear idea of what you're writing about, who you're writing to, and what your main 'call to action' is.

Summary

In this chapter we've looked at the importance of *planning your book* before you start. I think you can now see the reasons why it's so important to establish your niche, who you are writing for and why the 'call to action' needs to be clear and cohesive.

Planning the book out using pen and paper, mind-mapping software or Notepad then helps to gather all the information into one place and will help the book write itself. With a good plan, all you're doing is fleshing out each point until each bit is finished.

Simples!

Chapter 4

Mindset

"We all talk to ourselves. A major key to success exists in what we say to ourselves, which helps to shape our attitude and mindset."
- Darren L. Johnson

The '5 Mindset Attributes' That will Help you Complete Your Book.

In this chapter, we're going to be looking at the '5 Mindset Attributes' that will really help you in your writing project. Without them, you may find yourself starting with great enthusiasm, getting a few dozen pages written and then losing interest. Other more important tasks will suddenly pop up, and your writing will grind to a halt. (I've had my share of that happening too, so this is coming from a place of experience.)

If the foundation of 'I can do this' is not established before you begin, then you will find yourself stopping as soon as a bump or hurdle presents itself.

These five attitudes are simple and easy to adopt, but without them, your project will either never get finished, or even worse, won't get started. Thinking about writing a book is one thing, knowing and *believing* you can, will determine your success.

Let's go through these mindset attributes now, and then we can move onto 'Accountability' and 'Setting a deadline' next.

1. Having a 'can do' attitude

Before you start your writing project, it's essential that you get into the 'can do' attitude. Lots of people think that writing a book is extremely daunting and far too difficult, hence the reason why so few do.

Writing a book can be hard work if you skip the planning bit outlined in the last section. But if you get this bit done then writing the book is much, much easier.

Making the writing as easy as possible will help dissolve the feeling of it being hard work. We all love and gravitate towards the path of least resistance, and this is why planning the book is really smart. I know I keep going on about the plan... but without it, excuses will all too readily be used as to *why not* to write.

Committing to the project is also essential. Yes, it's going to take some time, but some of my clients have managed to write their book in less than 12 weeks, and that was just doing 30 minutes of writing a day. (Or 2 ½ hours a week, in one sitting.)

The clients that *aren't* successful are people who don't see the project as important. Their writing never gets done and they are full of excuses as to why.

Sometimes we can be our own worst obstacle. If you're finding yourself resisting getting started, then what is it that's causing that block? Is it time? Is it fear? Is it not being clear enough on what you're writing about? (It can even be a mix of all of these, and I'm going to confess that it took me a lot longer to publish this book than it should, so I'm no stranger to fear getting in the way of my publishing goal.)

Getting someone on board to help you could be the key to getting it done.

Writing a book doesn't have to take a huge amount of time, and having a *can do* attitude will really help. Every time you feel the fear, ask yourself, *"Is this book going to help people?"* If the answer is yes, then push your fear aside and keep going.

Step 1*: Get out of your own way.*

2. Believe in yourself and the value of your work.

This follows on from the last attribute; you must believe in your ability, and in the message you're writing about. You've done your research, and you have established your target audience – now it's time to share it.

Believing you have the knowledge and expertise is critical when writing a book. Without this you will find yourself doubting the project. And when other important projects spring up, suddenly your inner voice will start saying things like, "Well, I didn't really have anything important to say anyway", or "Who was I to think I could write a book…?"

Don't let that happen to your book project. Believe in yourself, and the value of your message.

3. Make your writing a priority

Some may argue that this is not an attitude, but it my eyes it is. It's essential that you see this project as a *high enough of a priority that it will not be put aside if something seemingly more important comes along.*

Unfortunately, a book does not have a voice, it's a silent scheme, which requires commitment and effort on the part of the writer – you!

Successful writers make writing enough of a priority for it to happen on a regular basis, and they prioritise it. Writers make a conscious decision to write, and it's this attitude that needs to be instilled at the very beginning.

Setting a date and having accountability can all help to cement your 'priority mindset'. Planning to the last detail, and having fantastic accountability is all well and good but without the mindset of 'this is important' and 'this must take priority', these plans can fall by the wayside when other projects or meetings wrestle for your time and attention.

I had to put a diary reminder in my Google calendar, so that I got an email, telling me it was 'writing time.' Just having this set up made a big difference. I then treated it like a customer - someone who I couldn't put off. You might find doing the same thing will really help with your scheduling.

4. Commit to writing and seeing it through

As I've already mentioned, writing a book takes commitment. I don't want to scare you off, but I have to be honest with you that this will take time. You must commit in order to see the project finished.

Without this attribute, starting will be easy, but staying on track could be an issue.

"There's a difference between interest and commitment. When you're interested in doing something, you do it only when circumstances permit. When you're committed to something, you accept no excuses, only results." - Tom Robbins

When you commit, *it's not a choice you make, it just is!*

 Top Tip: Some clients are able to book off a chunk of time – and they then go away and write – without the distraction of phones ringing, or staff needing their attention. Others put a name to the book – and treat writing it like seeing a physical client. These are super clever tactics to make sure your writing takes priority.

5. Just do it!

This ubiquitous quote from *Nike* really does encapsulate the next attribute so succinctly.

Without constant **action**, no amount of planning, adjustment of your mindset or setting up the greatest of accountability will get your book written.

Gaining the right tools, adopting the right attitude and committing to the project are of course essential, but nothing will be born of these traits if you then fail to ACT – therefore, *just do it.*

How you decide to do it is up to you and before the doubter in you starts saying things like… *"Oh I don't have time"*, remember this quote;

> *"Time is a created thing. To say 'I don't have time'*
> *is to say 'I don't want to.'"*
> **- Lao Tzu**

Accountability

Having accountability can dramatically increase your chances of becoming an author. Having someone help you with your plan, and setting an end date really helps cement your intention and makes it real. It makes it measurable and that is really important when embarking on a project that requires effort and commitment.

I've personally found that when I pay for someone to help me (be it a business mentor, or coach) then I really stick to what I set out to achieve. Paying for someone puts a value on what they're helping you with – so give this some food for thought when seeking out accountability.

Here are two quick ways to get accountability.

1. Tell someone/hire someone

A great tool that can help you become an author quickly and easily, is to either tell someone what you are planning, or adopt an accountability partner, someone that can hold you accountable and help you set deadlines for each section. Even if you just tell someone your plans, a magic combination of expectation and liability is then set, and it can help to keep you motivated and on track.

This person can be someone you work with, even your partner or spouse (if suitable), or you could *hire someone*. Book coaches and writing coaches are growing in popularity, and have the added bonus of knowing and understanding the frustrations of writing, as well as being able to give you hints and tips on how to keep the momentum going, with feedback along the way.

Also, the added element of hiring someone, which incurs a monthly cost, adds to the time factor. In other words, you will probably get the job done quicker and faster, knowing that each month an X amount of money is leaving your bank account.

If you decide that hiring a book coach is something that you are interested in, then you need to consider these few points before you proceed:

- ✓ Do they have experience in writing a book specifically for lead generation? Fiction is a different breed of book, and a coach who only has experience in this area might not be suitable, as they won't necessarily know the right tactics that a book used for lead generation requires.

- ✓ How many other books have they helped write before? Do they have examples?

- ✓ Can they help you with all aspects of your project, from planning, to brainstorming a strong 'call to action'?

- ✓ What access do you have to them? Will it be enough? Email is fine, but sometimes you just need to talk to someone as well.

- ✓ Have they written a book? How does it read? What was it used for?

The Book Refinery has helped numerous business owners get their books written and used effectively as a lead generation tool. Why not visit www.TheBookRefinery.com/testimonials to read how we have helped them, and then get in touch. We can have a quick, no obligation chat about your project. Simply email me at alexa@thebookrefinery.com

2. Set a deadline

Setting a date for when the book needs to be written by is a great tactic. If you don't, then the writing can go on for months, with no set deadline or cut-off point.

I encourage all of my clients to get a date in the dairy, a cut-off point that is set in stone, and unless something of extreme importance disrupts it, then this really helps in getting the writing done and finished on time.

Having no specific cut-off point set can cloud the mindset into thinking that this is of little importance, and adopting the 'commit to writing' attribute will seem half-hearted and flimsy.

Setting a date should be realistic. Don't give yourself too short a time period, just as you shouldn't spread it over too long a time period either. Stop and take a look at what is happening in your life. Where are you with regard to being able to commit time to this project? I also cover this in the '7-Step Process' so you don't have to think of a deadline now, just keep in mind that you will work more effectively and efficiently if you give this some thought, and plan a realistic cut-off time.

Don't however commit to this project if you are about to embark on some other life-changing challenge. If you're getting married in 2 months, planning on selling your house, or about to take on 10 new clients which will take up a lot of your time, then writing a book now might not be the best idea.

Wait until the situation is right, a space where you can dedicate some good quality time, then begin. Forward planning is advisable, but segmenting sufficient time is critical.

 Top Tip: I can honestly say, that the two most important aspects of writing and completing a book are; planning and accountability. Without these two steps, your book will be harder to write and less likely to be completed.

Summary

Getting into the right mindset and adopting the right attributes will really help you in your writing project. Understanding that fear can play a part in not getting your message out there can be quashed with knowing that your message is important.

Having a 'can do' attitude, along with commitment and a 'just do it' mentality will get your book written and published quickly and easily. Having accountability will help, and in some cases speed up the process. Writing can be a lonely task, but with the right help it can be made easier.

Setting a cut-off date also makes it real and is a great tactic to stay on track and on time. Combine all of the above and you're on the right path to becoming an author and producing one of the most successful lead generation tools available.

Chapter 5

The 7-Step Process

"Write in a diciplined manner, but write in a way that is natural to the individual's thought processes"
- Donald McKay

I have condensed the writing process down to seven simple steps. Each one can be done independently of the other, but I suggest you tackle and work through each one in order. However, you need to set yourself up for success before you start so that your book will be written quickly, simply and off to the printer within just a few months.

Setting Yourself up for Success

There are a couple of things you need to establish before you start that will really help you on your way to becoming an author within three months or less.

These 2 things are:

1. Choosing the right time to start the project

2. Establishing the best time of day to write.

Choosing the right time to start

As I said in the last chapter, don't try and accomplish writing a book if you have some other big project looming, like getting married or moving house. Writing does take discipline, and in order for your book to flow, I suggest you timetable a two to three month slot, and then follow the steps outlined below.

This is not to say that writing the book will take a solid 3 months to write (if that were the case, no business owner would be able to accomplish it) but it does require some dedicated time out of each day to write the required number of pages.

This is why establishing the number of pages you need to write first is really handy, as it puts it into a 'to do' type task, and can be slotted into your day's timetable.

Establishing the best time of day to write

Another very important aspect to consider is, when are you at your most creative?

Writing is a discipline that requires a certain amount of creativity. Knowing when you're at your most creative is really useful in order for the book to flow.

Are you best in the morning? If so, can you schedule a 40-minute slot in your diary in the morning, or whatever time period you need to write your required number of pages? Are you able to get up slightly earlier so that you can get into the office before the phone starts ringing, or emails start landing in your inbox? Turn off your web browser if you find yourself getting distracted!

Or, do you write better at night, when everyone has gone home? Whichever one it is (and you will find that you have a preference for one or the other) carve that time out of your schedule and fit in with your writing. You'll be amazed at how easy your writing becomes when you work with your natural flow.

You might find it easier to write all of your allocated pages for that week in one sitting, (rather than a bit each day) – some of my clients have found that segmenting a two hour chunk (or however long it takes you) much easier to stick to, and they then get all of their writing done in one go. Have a go at both, and see which one works for you but working against your creative rhythm will make your book stilted and difficult to read, and you will be inclined to give excuses as to why not to write, rather than be inspired to carry on.

The 7-Step Process

Below is 'The 7-Step Process' I have created to get your book written. I suggest you work through all the steps from one through to seven, completing each one fully before starting the next one.

Follow these seven easy steps, and you will have a book written and finished in no time at all. Read through them first before you start, and feel free to make notes along the way, or if you need to add any steps of your own, do so, just add them to the list and keep it handy when you start your writing.

Step 1. Brainstorming the title.

This can be done before you start, or as you're writing. However, having a working title is useful, as it keeps you on track and reminds you what your book is supposed to be about.

Jot down the three key things that your book is going to establish, and then come up with a benefit-style headline that identifies how the book will help your reader.

If you're finding this bit hard, then come up with four or five titles (the more the better) and then ask your client list which title they like best. Or run a split test with the two titles you think are the most beneficial and see which one wins. You may be surprised with the result. I did this with my book, and although I was convinced which title was going to win, the one I came up with last won, hands down!

Step 2. Create your 'Blueprint Plan'

This is one of the most crucial, if not *the most critical factor of your book* (see Chapter 3 about planning if you need a reminder). This is an overview of your project, created in such a way that all of your chapters and subheadings are defined. You just add your writing to each one and flesh out each point you have created in your plan.

Using the strategies outlined previously, you should spend a good amount of time planning your book, anything from 10 days to 2 weeks. Once you do, you'll find the writing process so much easier and your book will almost flow without effort.

Step 3. Set a date, and then work backwards

It's always a good idea to have a date set for when you want to have your book written. If you don't, then the project will never seem to have an 'end' and could go on for months.

One great tactic I employ, and encourage my clients to adopt is to calculate how many pages you need to write a day. A handy guide to make sure they're on track and to gauge how much time they need to spend on each section.

If you find yourself falling behind schedule, then either you've set yourself too short a time period, and you need to re-adjust, or you're not setting enough time each day to get your writing done. Either way, calculate what you need to change and then commit to that new schedule.

Step 4. Flesh out each section

This is where the rubber meets the road. You simply write more on each subheading that you've already defined in the 'Blueprint Plan'. You may need to go back to your blueprint and go into each node in more detail if you're finding this hard.

The more detail you can put into your plan, the easier it is to flesh out when you write your book. Once you have that established:

Get typing/or hit record.

Use any word-formatting programme to do this, BUT limit your use of page formatting. Simply use the formatting features to define the levels of subheadings. For instance the chapter title of your book will be Level 1. Then the subheading of that will be Level 2, and any other sub/sub heading of those, will be Level 3 (see my formatting guide where I explain this in more detail in Chapter 6).

I don't recommend going any further than 3 levels. If you need to have a fourth level simply use the bold feature of your word formatting programme. But remember try not to use too much formatting at this stage. You may be giving this to a typesetter who probably won't be able to copy any formatting that you have used, and if you spend ages trying to make your document look like a book (by using headers and footers for example) it will be a total waste of your time.

Of course using bold and italics is a good idea, as it will emphasise different aspects of your book, but don't get distracted with things like centreing the page numbers and creating margins, as this is the job of your typesetter and should be discussed at that stage of the process.

If you're recording your book, then make sure your 'Blueprint Plan' has enough detail so that you can just walk (or rather talk) through each point. If you get stuck, or you keep stumbling for words, then take another look at your plan. It might need more detail.

Also when you're recording your book, use your mouse to control the cursor on the mind-mapping software to highlight each section you're writing about, this way you won't get lost or forget which part you're talking about. If you make a mistake, don't panic. Either hit stop on the recording, or just keep going, giving clear instruction to the transcriber to edit the transcription.

If you're using Notepad, then just talk through your plan, using your cursor to step through each section, so you don't get lost (as to where you are).

Step 5. Review and refine.

Always review and refine your project as you go. If you feel that your 'Blueprint Plan' is not quite right, stop. Then tweak if necessary and carry on.

Just remember who your book is for, and what the 'call to action' is. I always find that having this typed up and in clear sight is really useful, as it keeps your mind focused on the end result and what you want the reader to do once they have read the book.

There is nothing wrong with editing your 'Blueprint Plan'. If after a few days, or few thousand words you realise that it's just not flowing, or not right, address the problem then. Your 'Blueprint Plan' should be the backbone of your book, and if it's not right, stop and fix it before you continue.

Once you have it finished to your requirements carry on and write until you have enough pages to produce a (minimum) 64-page book. See the page converter in the next chapter to see how many A4 pages you'll need to write for a demy size 64 page book (or more).

Step 6. Get your writing checked by a proof-reader or copyeditor.

Once you have your book written, and you've read it enough times that you feel it's ready to go to a professional, then get it read by a proof-reader or copy-editor. Don't skimp on this. There's nothing worse than reading a book with lots of grammatical errors, or spelling mistakes. It just looks unprofessional, and makes it harder to read.

You might know what you're trying to say, but your target audience might not. This is why it's critical to get it read objectively by one other person first, either in your industry or even your target reader.

Then, I highly recommend using a professional proof-reader. They will be able to tell you if your book needs any further editing. It's worth spending the extra money at this stage. It produces a much more professional product, and your readers are far more likely to respond to your 'call to action' if the book is clear and easy to read.

Step 7. Print and publish your book.

You will need to source a printer to get your book printed. Once it's been printed and delivered, you then need to market your book either using one of the strategies I have outlined in Chapter 7, or using one of your own methods. Of course, if you've decided to go down the traditional publishing route, the printing and marketing will be taken care of for you, so you won't need to worry about this step.

I go into much more detail about how to print and market your book in the next chapter, but it's important to remember to shop around for your printer. Get quotes, discuss your requirements and get a feel for how they will deal with you. If you're going to be managing this process yourself, then you need to make sure you have all the relevant information, like page sizes (to give to the typesetter) cover size and spine width (for the cover designer) and delivery date.

 I have created a self-publishing checklist that lists all the steps you need to complete if you're managing this process yourself. You can download it at www.thebookrefinery.com/resources/self-publishing-checklist/ and click on the Green 'Downloadable PDF Checklist'.

Summary

So there you are, the seven steps in a nutshell, and hopefully an easy to follow process to help you write your book. Use these steps in conjunction with the right mindset and accountability discussed earlier, and you will have your book written within 3 months or less.

With proper planning, I'm confident that your book will literally flow out of your head and onto the page. I look forward to seeing you published on sites like Amazon.com.

There really is nothing like a book to propel you to expert status. And to have 'author' beside your name is a great accomplishment. So let's get that book out of your head, and into print!

Of course managing this process yourself will take time. So why not get me to help you. I have helped many coaching professionals get their book to print, and into the hands of prospective customers quickly and easily. Simply email me at alexa@thebookrefinery.com with details of your project and I can then help you through the process.

Chapter 6

How to Publish Your Book

Amazon are in the business of making money. They are not in the business of making authors rich.

This chapter is divided into two sections. Section one is about the publishing process and Section two is about the layout and printing. Of course, if you decide to use the traditional publishing option, you can skip Section two, as this will be taken care of for you. However, you might want to check out the marketing section later on in this chapter. Traditional publishers will do some of the marketing for you, but they also expect you to do some as well.

Section 1 - Publishing

Before I begin to explain the different options you have, with regard to publishing your book, let me first explain what publishing is; publishing is no more than toning your work, be it audio, video, or written word into a form that is accessible by people other than yourself.

For years, people thought it was more complicated because only mainstream traditional publishers did it, and you rarely got to find out the process involved. Even as an author you didn't really know what was going on behind the scenes; you sent your manuscript to a publisher and twelve or eighteen months later you'd be sent a copy of a paperback book, and the whole process was a thorough mystery.

It's really only a combination of more accessible, cheaper, better print options, and the development of Internet selling (particularly Amazon) which has allowed publishing to be more accessible to writers, and people are far less frightened by it because 'want to be authors' are now given a lot more choice in publishing their work.

> *Publishing is no more than turning your intellectual property*
> *into a format that is accessible by your readers, your customers,*
> *your clients, whoever they may be.*
> **- Edward Peppitt, Author and Publisher**

When it comes to publishing your book, you basically have two choices:

1. Traditional publishing.

2. Self-Publishing

I will be explaining the differences between the two so that you have a real understanding of what each entails, but for books that are written for lead generation, I would recommend the second and I'll be explaining why within the course of this chapter.

Traditional Publishing

A traditional publisher is (and this is the vital distinction between the other options you have) a company that is going to take the entire risk of publishing your book. They pay for the editing, the typesetting, the proof-reading, the printing, the warehousing, the storage, the running costs and the shipping costs. This is usually around the £5,000 mark, so a traditional publishing company will be looking at what your book will be worth in terms of how many copies it will sell, and how much a return *they* will make on their investment.

Traditional publishers also have the contacts and resources to get your work into all the national branches of good bookshops, like Waterstones and WH Smith. Whereas if you self-publish, getting your book into book shops can be hard work, and in some cases, be impossible! So if getting your book into shops is paramount, then you should definitely explore this route.

When you want to get your book traditionally published, you can't approach publishers directly*, you have to go through 'literary agents' and they take your work to the publishers. There are 1000's of agents and thanks to the internet, most are at your fingertips. Each agent is usually a specialist in a particular genre, (I say usually, but some agents might represent more than one) be it children's books, self-help, sci fi and so on and it's really important you do your research before you approach any. Note; if your work is very niched, you might not find an agent who is that specific – so it's more researching ones that fit your ethos and broader genre. You can do this by finding out what books they like; (are they on Goodreads?) do they have social media – can you follow them? Then you can get a feel for what books they like, and who they read. Don't dismiss this step – as finding out what they like in terms of reading can be a really smart way of introducing yourself, as it shows that you've done your research.

When you've found your agent, you then need to find out what they want. Do they want a submission letter? Is there a specific proposal you need to fill out? Find that out first, and then you can tailor make your submissions to them. I wouldn't send out more than 8 submissions in a go – and remember 99% of them will be rejections. Have your hard hat on… these agents get sent 1000's of applications a day – and you can help yourself stand out by carefully following their guidelines; go off-piste, and your submission will find itself in the bin.

After extensive research and asking other people in the profession, there are some publishers that can be approached directly. This is more common in non-fiction titles and business style books. It's not something I would advocate – but thought I would add it as a note. There are hundreds of publishing houses, and to say none of them like to be approached directly is a bit presumptuous. However, I would say it's more common practice to go through an agent.

Pros – if you find yourself with a publishing deal – congratulations! Your book will now be published by a publisher, and you will be making money from selling the book. They will now edit, lay out, and print the book for you, they will even advertise it, and get it in book shops ready for your reader. You will have a contract in place (maybe for more books) and they will be your publisher. How you get paid, depends on the contract.

It could be:

→ **A flat fee**; an agreed amount, that stays the same no matter how well the book sells.

→ **Royalties**; a small amount, for each book sold, and

→ **An advance against royalties**; an amount up front, and then additional amount, depending on the book sales.

But remember you're getting a royalty on the amount received by the publisher – so although your book is selling for £10, the amount the publisher gets for that book could be as little as £5 (even lower if a big distributor is squeezing 65% discount) – so it's whatever % of that price – not the cover price. Royalties can be as little as 10% – so that's 50p per book…. Not as much as you might have originally thought. This might be a real deal breaker for you – so look over the contract carefully.

Cons – You will need to sign a contract, and they may want to change the direction of your book, and you may only be making pennies per book sold. (Remember, they are in the business of making them money first, not you!) They might only offer you a yearly contract – and could drop you the following year if your sales aren't high enough – if you're not making them money, don't expect them to keep you on their books! Be careful what you sign in the contract – read the small print. You don't want to find yourself with no rights to your work when your publishing contract comes to a close.

It's notoriously hard to get a publishing deal and you can expect to spend a lot of time doing the research, and submitting letters. All of this time is not paid for, so think carefully and be prepared for a long road ahead.

If you really believe in your book, then being persistent, resilient and patient is key. You may also find that self-publishing is a good first step and I outline why in my authors' Tip below.

Alternatives – Self publishing.

If you feel that traditional publishing is the best option for your book, then the top three tips that I recommend are:

1. Stop writing your book and work on your proposal

2. Establish what your book is about, and who the book is aimed at in 150 words or less

3. Identify why YOU are the best person to write this book (as in, what gives you authority and experience to write what you are writing).

Interesting to see that this process requires you to identify your target audience; it seems niching is vital for this process, and it just backs up what I've said at the beginning of the book – know who your target audience is!

Update – The information in this section was also published as a blog post on The Book Refinery and I got some really useful feedback from a reader. They suggest, when you get your contract, make sure you get it checked over by a professional. Don't rush to sign; if it looks too good to be true, it probably is!

Self-Publishing

If traditional publishing is not for you, or you've tried the above with little result and feel that you want to do it yourself, then self-publishing has come on leaps and bounds. You can now self-publish your book fairly quickly and cheaply, depending on your route.

What is self-publishing compared to traditional publishing?

Self-publishing is where you produce and print your book yourself – you fund the entire process. You will need to get an ISBN number (the special bar code that is put on the book cover; this allows you to sell your book online and in book shops) and you generally become the publisher. (I say generally, as there are third party companies where you can buy ISBN numbers and they will then be the publisher – my sister company, compass-publishing.com is one of them. We don't take any royalties from your book, we're just there to help you get your book published.)

Sounds wonderful right? Well, in essence, yes. However, there are now 1000's of self-published authors out there, and as much as that is good… you don't really want to appear 'self-published' – or rather you want to make sure your book looks just as inviting as a traditional published book does – and that is quite tricky if you're doing it all yourself. You've not only got to get your book edited and proofread, (I **ALWAYS** recommend you get it professionally edited and if you are submitting your work through agents, for the traditional publishing then this will need to happen anyway) you then need to lay it out, get a cover designed and get it printed. Knowing who to use can be a minefield, and if you're not careful pricey.

Editing and proof reading

This will be one of the most expensive elements of book production, and something you will need to do yourself. Although if you're trying to get your book traditionally published, then you'll need to get your work edited as well, before you submit it to an agent.

Layout and cover design

Now, there are lots of 'do it yourself' layout options for you – I know that CreateSpace offer templates that you can use, (you simply stream in your Word document into the template) and this could well be the right option for you. But not all templates are necessarily the right fit – for instance, if you've written a business book that requires a specific layout, with pictures and graphs or pull out boxes and fancy quotes, getting the help of a professional book designer is highly recommended. Also, think of how many other people have used the same template as you. If you've written a novel, then that probably isn't such a worry, as most layouts are pretty standard, but if you want your book to be different, then is looking like hundreds of other books the right choice for your work?

The same goes for cover design. I've seen a huge rise in the 'do it yourself' free software that is available and if you're strapped for cash this could be just the ticket – BUT if you're not sure what you're doing, then your book can scream self-published. It's the little nuances that can make a huge difference – and these mistakes are the most common:

→ **Line spacing** - this is the biggest give away.

→ **Font choice** - do you want your book jacket to have the same font that 100's of other people have used on their cover? Also, lots of people use too many types of fonts and it looks really unprofessional and…

→ **Text placement** – how you place your text on the cover needs some thought and understanding (I've seen do-it-yourself cover design where the title of the book, the author's name and picture are all jostling for attention, and seem confusing and inharmonious) – whereas professional cover designers know exactly how to get this right.

Remember, you're a writer... *not a book designer* and feeling that you have no other option when you're self-publishing your book is a mistake. If you can, **hire a professional** to design your cover. I know it's an added expense, but your cover needs to represent your book; we all do really judge a book by its cover!

Competition in 2017 is just too great to cut corners in time or money, and an automated jacket design will stick out like a sore thumb.

Pros – You are your own publisher and all the money you earn from the book is yours. So if you're selling your book directly, then your cover price is what you earn.

You have complete control over how your book is produced, printed and distributed. You call the shots, so if you need to find out who is buying your book – this is an ideal option. However, if you're self-publishing only through CreateSpace, then Amazon will be selling your book, and they won't provide you with this information – and for authors of books that are being used for lead generation, this might not be the best option.

Also, it seems that big publishing houses are interested in authors who have self-published. I know editors at mainstream publishers who spend as much time looking at sales data of self-published books as they do reading through submissions from authors and agents – so this is something to consider.

Cons – It's expensive, as you are taking on all of the production and marketing costs. This includes editing, layout, cover design, printing and distribution. Of course printing through POD printers can seem like a cheaper alternative, but do read my info below to see exactly what you're signing up for if you go this route. It may seem tempting – but is it really that cost effective?

Alternatives – You might find yourself using a publishing company that is specific for self-published authors, like compass-publishing – they provide support and help for your publishing project, but don't necessarily take any monies from your book. Of course they don't pay any advance for your work (see above) but they can offer a one stop solution if you need help with all of the elements of self-publishing. There are quite a few companies out there that offer this sort of support, so check out their small print and see how they can help you.

Please see the table at the end of this chapter for comparative services and benefits of each type of publishing option. Also, if you're self-publishing you'll need to print your book as well – see below for your options.

 If you are still undecided on which option is best for you, then write down what it is you want the book to do (refer back to Chapter One, 'How to use your book') and be really honest with yourself. Do you want to be 'published' for the sake of it, or do you want to use this book as a powerful lead generator?

If it's the latter, then self-publishing is your answer. Just be careful if you use a self-publishing company, as you can find yourself restricted with this option as explained previously.

If you're STILL uncertain which option is right, then read these top three myths that are associated with publishing, they make for interesting reading!

The top 3 myths about publishing:

→ **Myth #1**. Traditional publishing will do all the marketing for you and will make you a best seller.

No, the publisher will do a small focused, cheap marketing campaign. A single marketing campaign could cost up to £5,000. Add to that the initial investment of £5,000 for the printing and editing costs and that's £10,000 on a book that costs £10. Amazon buys it at a 60% discount, which is then £4.00. It's cost them £2.00 to print, with 40p to the author. How many books do you need to sell to get that original £10,000 back?

Quite a few!

This is why the publisher will still rely on the author's platform to be strong and to sell books as well.

Also, the number of books that need to be sold to reach 'best seller' levels are in the *many thousands per week.*

→ **Myth #2**. You will make money on the **front-end sales.**

This is relevant for any publishing option. You might get 10% on royalties, which equals to about 40p a book for traditional publishing. The book seller will be getting the largest amount, so in fact there is very little money to be made by using a traditional publisher.

If you're self-published, you could make £4.00 on each book (or whatever you're charging your customers to buy a copy) but if you've used print on demand and it's costing you £3.50 per unit, you're not going to be making any decent amount of money on the front end.

This is why using a book for setting up your back end services can be very smart, as it's there where you will make your money.

→ **Myth #3**. Just because you've written a book, it will **sell itself.**

No it won't, you still have to market your book to your target audience, just like you would with any other marketing exercise. Even when using a traditional publisher, they will expect a certain amount of effort from you to sell your book, especially if it's a business book directed at a targeted group of readers.

So, in summary, these are the two options available to you. Choosing which option is important. Be clear as to what you want the book to do, and then make a decision based on that. Also, feel free drop me an email at alexa@thebookrefinery.com if you want to discuss any of the options I have explained.

Just remember, there is one thing that I can guarantee when you *do get your book published*, and that is your readers and colleagues will revere you as an expert, as you've taken the time to commit to a writing project and imparted your knowledge by publishing your work.

The reverence of being knowledgeable about a subject and being disciplined enough to sit down and write about it, is why people perceive authors so highly.
~ Ed Peppitt, Author and publisher

Section 2 – Layout and Printing

If you've gone for the traditional option, then you can skip this bit! (Although you might want to find out what happens to your book if you get a traditional publishing deal.)

So, you're going to publish yourself. One thing to note if you decide on this route is, you're going to have to be very organised and be able to communicate to all your service providers, e.g. typesetter, designer and printer simultaneously so that the project runs smoothly. Also, do read the bit about printing after this section, as some printers offer you templates that you can use, so some of the information I've explained below might not be necessary.

I suggest you source your printer FIRST as you will be working with them to see what size book they can produce (you need to give these dimensions to your typesetter) plus you will need to know your spine width. Now this is quite tricky, as you need to know the number of pages your book is going to be, and you won't know that until you've decided your size of book.

Once you have a book size in mind, and decided on paper quality (what thickness of paper you use will affect your spine width too!) then you need to relate all that information to your cover designer.

This may seem very complicated but it's easy when you get yourself organised.

I've created a self-help checklist, which is available on my website. I've numbered the actions you need to do in order, so that you know what you need to do and when. When you self publish, there are quite a few steps to consider, so use this checklist to keep you on track. Simply follow this link www.thebookrefinery.com/resources/self-publishing-checklist/ and click on the green 'Downloadable PDF Checklist'

Layout - Design and Style

As with any creative project, you will no doubt have given some thought as to how you want your book to look once it's finished. During the writing process I suggest you don't spend a lot of time formatting your book (where you change font styles, margins, page numbers, headers and footers etc.) as this is just a distraction and you want your writing out of your head first.

The only formatting you do require when typing your book is heading levels, and any words or phrases you want to emphasise (use bold text or italics for this).

Heading levels explained

Most books only require a heading level structure of 3. Chapter titles are Level 1, the sub heading of that, is Level 2, and then any other smaller headings are a Level 3. (I also have different formating for Introduction, Contents, Foreword etc - and I just label that the name of the page)

Here is an example (using my book as an illustration):

Chapter 1 - Why Have a Book?

(The title of the chapter is usually always a Level 1)

Using a Book for Lead Generation

(A sub topic of that chapter is then a Level 2)

The 3 possible strategies:

(And a sub category of a Level 2, is then Level 3)

I don't suggest you go any further than three heading levels, but if you need to make something clear that is a sub category of a Level three, then just use the bold feature.

When you create your contents page, most typesetting programs allow you to choose how many heading levels you want to include in your contents. Once you've chosen how many levels you want to include, it will then generate a table of contents for you, very handy! I usually stick with two levels, but if your book is quite small, and consequently your contents page looks rather short, include the Level three headings as well.

Once you have your heading hierarchy sorted, just use the italic or bold feature for various words you want to emphasise.

 Design Tip: Don't go overboard with bold and italics! It can detract from what you are trying to emphasise. If every other paragraph has boldening, italicising, and underlining, it just shouts 'amateur' and the reader will become oblivious to what you're trying to emphasise.

Your typesetter can then do all the fancy headers and footers, and set up the side margins and page numbers for you.

If you're planning on typesetting your book yourself, then I do suggest you use a specific desktop publishing programme, like QuarkXpress or Adobe InDesign. They are specifically designed programmes with book layout features, that you just can't do (or are very tricky) in programmes like Microsoft Word. However, the latest Microsoft Word software is much easier to use, so give it a go if you have time on your hands, but be prepared to spend a good 2 to 3 weeks getting your book formatted correctly, or even longer if you're going to be using a programme you're not familiar with. Also, one thing of note: If you want to get your book formatted for Kindle, or any other e-reader, then having a Word copy of your book is very useful if you're going to convert this yourself. Or ask your typesetter what they can do in order for your files to be easily converted.

Questions to ask your designer

If you are going to be using a typesetter, then here are a few things you might want to consider before you hire one (the typesetter should ask you these questions when taking on your project. If they don't, then source another one).

→ **What is the style of your book?** (Genre)

Depending on what your book is about, then you should get a feel for how the book should look once it's finished.

Who is your book directed at? Who is the target audience? This should then give you some clues as to the style and feel of the layout and choice of font.

→ **What other books do you like?**

Which books do you find interesting to read, or engaging to the eye? If there are specific books that you do like, then take a look at their formatting. What features do you like? Make a note of them and then discuss these with your typesetter. It's much easier to get the right feel for your book when you have some ideas in mind.

Layout can really aid the readability of a book. This can include simple elements like font choice and the heading structure (already discussed). You might like to include margin tabs as well, especially if the book is quite complex and has many different sections that might get lost with simple heading titles.

Here are some other design elements that you should give some thought to:

Font

The type of font you use can really change the style and tone of your book, so it is worth giving this some thought. The general rule is that a serif font (a font that has tiny curlicues on the ends of the letters) is easier to read that a sans serif font which doesn't.

Example of Serif and Sans serif fonts

Serif fonts include:

- Times New Roman

- Palatino Linotype

- Cambria

Sans serif fonts include:

- Arial
- Calibri
- **Impact**

Being a typesetter myself, I always try to typeset my client's books in a serif font (although I do use a contrasting sans serif for heading titles).

Before you think of changing the rule, think of this: of all the new fonts that are now available, isn't it interesting that most printed national newspapers use Times New Roman as their typeface?

Also, if you are going to use a less common font for your book, do check with your typesetter that they have a copy. Most publishing programmes come with an array of font styles, but some of the more special ones might not be included. My advice is to choose a more common font. Trying to make your book stand out with something that is unfamiliar or different, could put readers off, so do give this some thought and talk it over with your typesetter, they should be able to offer some advice and guidance.

Header/ Footer

Header

This is the text that appears at the top of each page. The general rule is that the title of the book is on the left, and the chapter title is on the right. You can have different elements added, like have the title of the book in SMALL CAPS or use wingding icons either side of the book title, ⁓Title of Book⁓.

You might even like a line under your header, before the rest of the text then starts.

TITLE OF BOOK

The best way to navigate all of these is to look at lots of other books and use them for inspiration. However, don't get carried away. Over formatting a book can also be very distracting and make it look too fussy, so do use these design elements with caution.

Footer

This is usually the page number. You should generally use the same font as the header. There is no hard or fast rule as to whether the page number should be at the bottom, on the left or right, or in the middle, or at the top of the page, although I always think that if it's a more techy type book then the page number should be justified left or right. Subsequently, any book that has more of a story, or autobiographical feel should have the page number in the middle, but that is just my opinion and you can have your page number wherever you like.

Johnson Boxes

These are text boxes that are used to emphasise a fact, or could be used if giving a case study example. Generally they are outlined and have a slightly darker background colour and can be very effective at highlighting an important fact, or separating text. I used one on page 36

> These are Johnson boxes and you can use them to make text really stand out.

Johnson boxes are also a great way of directing the reader's eye and so are best used when there is something of real importance to highlight. You can even stylise the Johnson box with an icon, to really emphasise the point. I did a Johnson box recently, where the author had a 'soap box', so we boxed it out and had a little icon to show him on his 'soap box'. It really added to the style of the book, and gave some humour and consistency to his 'soap box' speeches.

Note: Microsoft Word will be really difficult to do this type of formatting, one of the many niggles that irritate me about the program. This is why I really recommend using a proper desktop publishing programme.

'Call to action' Boxes

Using a specially designed 'call to action' box is a great way of differentiating the 'call to action' from other parts of your text. Using a picture icon alongside it is also a great little design tip, and one I use for my clients as well as my book.

You will want to make these boxes different from any Johnson boxes you use. It doesn't have to even be in a box. See this example I used recently. I've changed the text slightly, but you can see how the graphic works with the box.

To find out more information about this strategy, then visit **www.websitehere.com**

I just indented the text, with a little computer/mobile graphic and this really stands out.

> If you are going to use icons, then make sure you have copyright permission to use them. You can either design them yourself, get a designer to do it for you, or use a stock photography website like iStock.

Number of pages

Now this may not seem like a design element, however design can come into play here, so you might want to give this some thought at the design stage.

When you get your book printed the number of pages is important. Traditional printing uses page blocks of four. (It used to be 16, which is quite a lot) but digital presses have come a long way, and you can have a much smaller page count, and still have a proper 'spine'. You want to aim for a minimum number of 64, otherwise your book will look more like a 'glorified pamphlet'

So if you need to 'add' pages to your book, then fiddling around with design elements can help.

Here are a few elements you can tweak;

- ✓ Font selection (choose a wider style font like Cambria)
- ✓ Margin sizes
- ✓ Separate section pages (this will add 2 pages, as you need a blank opposing page)
- ✓ Use of Johnson Boxes.

However, you can only tweak so much, and it would almost be impossible to make 20 pages of text equal a 64-page book, so you would need to add more content.

Of course the size of your book will have an effect as well. I like to use Demy size (216mm x 138mm) and roughly one and a half pages of A4 (Times New Roman, 12 point - Microsoft Word default size of a document) equals about two pages of Demy (depending on your inside and outside margins, as well as your header and footer margins) but this is something you will need to discuss with your typesetter. They should be able to help you with little design tweaks that can add pages if needed.

Of course, there are elements that should always *stay the same*, and not be messed with. For a professional looking book, then I suggest the following:

Elements you shouldn't tweak

- ✗ How the text is aligned. The most professional looking format is justified, where the text is square to the right edge, rather than a raggedy appearance.

✗ Having too big a space between lines. (I think this looks unprofessional and can make your book seem lightweight, however some clients have insisted I do this, to give their text room to breathe, so it's a personal choice.)

✗ Using a font bigger than 12 point. NO! (I don't like using font over 11.5 myself.)

Your Book Cover

Book cover design is a profession in itself, and unless you are a graphic designer, then trying to create your book cover will be a lengthy process. There are certain rules you need to know in order to create a professional looking cover, and I would highly recommend you leave this to a cover designer (or ask if your typesetter does cover design too). Getting this element right is important. People really do judge a book by its cover, although interestingly enough, almost double the amount of time is spent looking at the back of the cover rather than the front. So bear that in mind when designing your jacket.

Limit your colour palette to just two or three, and if you have company colours or a logo then this is a great place to use them.

Make the title of the book the main element of the design. Sometimes using just text can be really effective. If you're really stuck, then take a look at some of the book covers on Amazon; it's a great resource for inspiration, and can really help you come up with some good ideas which you can then discuss with your designer.

If you're going to use a graphic, then just like the inside of the book, make sure you have the correct copyright permissions.

Design Tip: Use the font you use on the cover as a subheading font inside your book. This then creates some continuity.

There are *lots of* 'DIY' cover templates available - Canva is probably the biggest one, and although it's great for people on a budget, templates have one big draw back, and that is, other people will use them too. Also, I can spot a Canva cover a mile away - the spacing between the text is too big (imo) and the fonts are ubiquitous. Be really careful before you think of using one of these 'designed for you, all you do is add text' type of templates. 1000's of other people are doing the exact same thing!

Back Cover

A good back cover should include a punchy synopsis along with teasing-style bullet points as to what the book is going to include.

If you can get any testimonials about your book, then this is the ideal place to show them off. In fact the last book I worked on, the entire back cover was purely testimonials, and it worked really well in persuading people to buy it. Remember how I spoke about testimonials earlier on - Accountant #1 vs. Accountant #2? This is where getting testimonials really comes into play. Just remember, if you're going to use a testimonial on your book cover, then it needs to be about the BOOK… not general ones about your service.

Great ways of getting these is to give people a pre-printed copy (PDF) of your book, and ask them for a testimonial, in return for you giving them a free copy. Then select the best testimonials from your replies.

I always encourage a picture of the author to go on the back cover as well. It engages 'trust' and allows the reader to see that you are real. A short biography can then be included next to the picture.

Figure 3 - An example of About the Author

Elements to include on the back cover:

✓ Photo of the author

✓ A good synopsis (with bullet points) of what the reader will find out inside the book

✓ A short biography of the author

✓ An ISBN number

✓ Price

✓ Website address.

✓ Testimonials if applicable

So, that's the insides sorted... now it's time to get your book printed.

Printing

Printing your book is now the next step. Whoever you print with, be it CreateSpace, Lulu.com or traditional printers, you will need to have print ready PDF's. These are high resolution documents that don't move or flow. They are stapled down so to speak, so that whatever screen (or device) opens this, it will always look the same (unlike Word, where it ebbs and flows like the tide). It's really important you know this difference. Now some of the companies above will offer a free uploading system, where you can take your Word document and stream it into one of their templates and then export it as a PDF – this can be really convenient, but like I've stated before, not always the best option for your book. Do you want your book to look like everyone else's? What if there is a problem with uploading? Also, if you use CreateSpace and use their 'free ISBN' service, you cannot then use these documents to print elsewhere.

You will also need to have your cover ready. However, before you finish your cover, you need to know which printer you're going to use, because you will need to have a spine width measurement – and that all depends on the paper you use, and the page count. Again, companies like CreateSpace have templates that you can use and they have a width calculator that determines the size of the spine, BUT – if you're not used to formatting Word to a good level I can guarantee you're going to struggle. Covers are very specific when setting up margins and bleed within the document, (so that the text doesn't run off the page) and I've seen some good cover design on screen look awful on the printed book, as the spacing around the edges has not been enough – even though it was designed within the margins – not enough extra space was allowed within the document itself.

Types of printers

POD

Print on Demand (or POD) is where your book is printed as someone orders it. Companies like CreateSpace, Lulu and Ingramspark are all POD printers. CreateSpace is part of the Amazon group, and if you publish your book through them, your book is then listed on their platform. This may seem fantastic – BUT look at the cost. Yes, it costs you nothing up front, but the royalties you earn will be very little – they take a hunk of commission for printing and distributing your book, (obvs) so if you sell your book for say £5.99 – you will receive roughly £1.20 in royalties per book. Click here to see their royalties' charges. And that doesn't get paid to you for 3 months. (Their invoicing system is so complicated!)

Lulu.com works out to be a cheaper option – but their quality is not fantastic (imo) – and it takes over 8 weeks for them to distribute to Amazon. Imgramspark is also a big contender and this article shows the difference of royalties earned between CreateSpace and Ingram.

It's really important to know ALL of these figures. I think authors are so quick to 'publish' their book, and in the easiest way possible, they don't actually do the MATHS. Earning so little for your hard work really makes me cross – but authors seem to think there is no other option or are not willing to do the research to find out what option is best for them.

Also, if you're trying to get any of the POD books into bricks and mortar shops, it'll be tough. Most book shops don't take POD books – as there is a no return policy. (And it seems in the States, that quite a few book shops are boycotting CreateSpace imprinted books – see ISBN allocation for what imprint means– so it's really important to find out all of these facts FIRST.) However, you can order your own copies of your book (usually at a special price) and you can then offer these to the book stores – but don't forget, they'll want a discount which can be as high as 40% on the cover price (some want 65%!).

Examples of POD – CreateSpace, Ingramspark, Lulu etc.

Pros – Cheap to set up (Although, you might want to note that Ingram has a set-up and yearly fee. Amazon have a yearly fee to sell your books.) You can upload your book, and make changes and you have the Amazon distribution network in which to sell your book. You don't need to distribute books yourself – it's all done for you! This could well be the best option for fiction writers – although I would add a caveat to get your book cover professionally done.

Cons – I don't think the quality is as good as traditionally printed books. You have to do all of the uploading yourself, and you pay a hefty price for the pleasure. The biggest con for me is the chunk of money they take. Please do your maths before you decide.

Alternatives – Traditional printing.

Traditional Printing

Traditional printers are usually bricks and mortar printers who print more than 25 copies of your book in one go. You then order X number of copies, and they then get delivered to your door. I believe these are better quality than the POD books, but it's all a matter of opinion. If you're printing more than 1,000 books, then it's more than likely the printer will use a 'litho' press, and that without a doubt is better than digital (which is what POD uses) – although to be fair digital presses have come a long way in terms of quality.

Traditional printers will give you more paper choice, and the cover stock is heavier (that means it won't bend so easily). The printer I use, uses eco-friendly sourced paper as well which is important to me. I also get to speak to a proper person (try doing that with Amazon!) and this could be really helpful for a first timer.

You will need to have your files ready for print – (High Res PDF files I spoke about earlier) and there are some printers who will do the layout for you (bonus!) but find out what books they have done, and always get a proof copy – I've had to rescue several books that were laid out by a printer and they weren't great (they just gave the author less to worry about).

Finding printers is relatively easy; just do a Google search (although if you can find one through a recommendation, even better) and ask questions. You'll usually find a helpful team, and you should expect your book printed within 10 days. Always get a proof first – so that you can see exactly how it looks when it's printed. Most printers will allow corrected PDF's to be sent (some might charge an additional fee for this but mine don't.) Seeing your book physically in your hands is a must for new authors – it's amazing to see how different the book looks in terms of layout – and if you're not experienced in book layout, your proof copy will show you just how it all translates.

Pros – If you are using a book where you need to know the details of the person buying it (books written for marketing purposes and lead generation) then I would absolutely recommend the traditional route.

The cost per *unit* is cheaper. This difference really comes into force on the number of copies you print up front. The more copies you print, the cheaper the unit price becomes – but no matter how many copies you order from Amazon, it will always remain the same. So, if you print traditionally, even though you're paying for postage, you'll make more money per copy than if you sell only through Amazon. (Also, as a note, if you want to order 'author copies' through Amazon, they will be printed and shipped from the States which means a hefty postage cost. You can get around this, by lowering your price of your book on Amazon.co.uk itself, ordering copies through .co.uk site, and then once the order is confirmed, put your price back up – but this seems a real faff!)

Remember, Amazon will not let you know who's bought the book, so if that information is important to you, then selling it this way is not smart.

"Amazon is in the business of making money,
not to make authors rich."

Cons – It's pricey up front, (but cost per book is much lower) and you have to do all the fulfilment yourself (this might be a pro though if you need this info). Storing 100's of books might not appeal - although there are fulfilment houses that can do all of this for you – but you are looking at an additional expense.

Alternatives – If you can afford it, I would do both. Get your book traditionally printed, and upload onto Amazon. Then you can really compare the price – and see which one works for you.

Authors' Tip! Also, more and more print houses are offering POD style print runs – at a much cheaper price than before. So, getting just 25 copies is much more affordable – and you don't have to buy in the 1000's. The best advice is to do your research, ask around and get lots of quotes and samples. It may seem like a lot of work up front, BUT generally when you find a printer that you like, you stick with them.

Oh and one last word of warning: Don't, and I mean DON'T set your publicity date/book launch UNTIL you have the books sitting in your garage/storage facility. All sorts of things can happen between an 'estimated' delivery date, and the books ACTUALLY being delivered. I've heard too many stories of people organising their book launch, with no books in their possession, just a 'delivery date' marked in their calendar, with disastrous results.

It's a big mistake!

Who is the Publisher?

This is quite complex, but it's important to know. It all depends on who 'owns' the ISBN number. This is the 13 digit 'identification' number that is printed on the back cover. You can buy ISBN numbers directly from the ISBN agency: Nielsen in the UK and Bowker in the States. These ISBN numbers will then belong to you – and you can be listed as a publisher for your work. You have an option of buying 1, 10 or 100. If you buy 1, you're looking at around £98.

You can also buy ISBN numbers from other third party brokers, (like printers and other self-publishing companies) but they will then become the publisher of your book – and you need to make sure if they have anything in place to 'tie you in', or if they relinquish rights to your work. So, for instance, if you get a publishing deal through Bantam, they will use one of their ISBN numbers, and Bantam will be the publisher of your book. You will also have a contract in place, which states how much money you will make from each book (called royalties) and how long they will be your publisher for (usually it's dealt in terms of years.) There are some brokers who sell ISBN numbers (like Compass-publishing.co.uk) who waive all rights to your work, don't tie you into a contract, but are there to just help you through the ISBN number buying process – it's expensive, and can take up to 10 working days – but do check carefully what their small print entails.

There are options to buy ISBN numbers from the POD companies that I have mentioned – CreateSpace have several options – and if you go with their 'free one' then CreateSpace Independent Publishing Platform will be listed as the publisher and "This ISBN can only be used with the CreateSpace Independent Publishing Platform." So you can't distribute your book in any other way! You can choose to upgrade and get a paid for ISBN number – $99 at time of writing, and then YOU become the publisher and distribute how you like.

If you do buy your own ISBN number, you will then be responsible for listing that number with whichever agency you bought it from. This is really important, as in the UK it's a legal requirement to submit books to the libraries (The British Library) once your book is printed, and if you don't register your book, bookshops and retailers will not know any information about it. If you've bought your ISBN number from a broker, they may do this for you (Compass-publishing does) so you need to check when you order.

If you don't have an ISBN number, then you won't be able to sell on Amazon and other online stores.

Summary

Typesetting your book correctly is critical. It can add professionalism and help the reader understand what it is you're trying to tell them.

Try not to get too caught up with fancy design elements that make your book look fussy or hard to follow. Stick to proven guidelines (like a serif font) and always get the correct copyright permission for any images you use.

There are numerous design elements that I haven't covered (I could write an entire book on the subject!) but if you want to find out more, then I highly recommend 'Elements of Style' by William Strunk Jr. and E. B. White, and 'Type and Layout' by Colin Wheildon. Both are available on www.Amazon.co.uk.

However, if you simply don't have time to think about each of these specific components, then make sure you choose a typesetter who understands the basics. Typesetting your book will use up a large chunk of your production costs, so you need to make sure that they can deliver a professional looking book, and in a timeframe that suits you.

The same goes for the cover design too. Leaving the style entirely up to the designer is both dangerous and not very helpful to the designer. Think of WHO your target audience is, and go from there. Think really hard about using free book design software – it's easy to spot, and do you want your cover looking like everyone else's?

Also, spend a good amount of time researching your printer. Use someone who you've heard good things about. Don't necessarily go for the cheapest option, they are probably cheap for a reason!

Of course if you want to self-publish, but don't want to outsource all the different elements that a self-publisher needs, then get in touch with The Book Refinery. We can take care of all of these elements for you. Simply visit www.thebookrefinery.com for more information, or get in touch. Email me at info@thebookrefinery.com and tell me a bit about your project.

Chapter 7

Marketing Your Book

If you've gone down the traditional publishing route, then most of the marketing will be taken care of for you. However, they will expect you to do some marketing yourself.

This will require you to 'tell your prospective readers' about your book. You'll need to network, and find out where your readers are. This can include what type of magazines they read, or what websites they visit.

Book marketing is no different from any other type of marketing. Just being 'published' isn't enough. You need to let people know about it, and having it displayed on a bookshelf won't be enough either!

That said, I find a great way of promoting a book, is to use it as a 'free giveaway'. Now don't gasp, and fall off your chair.

"Give my book away for free… are you kidding?" – no, I'm not!

As I've already established in Chapters One and Six, writing a book to make money on the front end of sales is almost impossible. Unless you are planning on selling 10,000 copies, you won't get rich quick or make any significant money on the front-end sales.

So, giving the book away for free (or using one of the three strategies I outline below) your calls to action, which are scattered throughout the book, should be strong and compelling enough, so that you will make money on the back end services that you offer.

This is why it's critical that your book is written in the way that I've explained. You need to impart enough information so that the reader wants to learn more, and by that I mean visit your website, or contact you for follow-up services.

It's a very effective tactic. You will find that people will be very happy to receive a free book, and in the meantime you will be establishing yourself as an 'expert' because you're a published author.

Using your book as a way of getting more targeted people into your sales funnel is one of the smartest tactics you can use, and I've outlined the 3 ways my clients have used their books to achieve this.

Using your Book for Lead Generation

Here are three ways of using your book for lead generation. Just remember whichever option you choose (and you could come up with a strategy of your own) make sure the process is simple. Explain why the prospect needs to read your book, and ensure the follow up sequence naturally leads the reader to the next step.

The 3 possible strategies:

1. **Free download of the book** (provided as a PDF) – with an opportunity to get the physical book for free (*just pay for P&P*).

2. **Free download of the first 2 chapters** (provided as a PDF) – with an opportunity to get the rest of the physical book for the full price (or a special offer, like free P&P or at a discount).

3. **Free download of the contents** (like the 'look inside' feature on Amazon.com) – with an opportunity to get either the full PDF download or physical copy for full price.

These strategies talk about using lead pages.

Lead pages: A quick overview.

'Lead pages' are a specific type of webpage that stand alone from your main website. Their purpose is to elicit one response: for the visitor to submit their name and email address.

They are very popular and when set up properly, can be very effective at doing this. There are many different software options to create these pages just Google 'Lead page' or 'squeeze page' software and have a look.

So let's look a little closer at each strategy and how they have worked for other clients.

1. Free download – with opportunity to get the physical book for free, only paying a small P&P amount.

This is one of the most common strategies that my clients have used. It's simple, easy and is a great way of getting a prospective customer's name and email address. It's like the ultimate 'Free Report' offer you see on many websites and lead pages, and let's face it, who can resist a free book?

It's a simple formula; you create a specific page on your website (a lead page is the best example) and create a short sales piece of what your book is all about and what the reader will learn. You then offer them the opportunity to submit their name and email address, in return for the free download (a PDF version of your book) and once they have registered their details they then get sent the free download.

On the following download page (make sure your lead site software provides you with this feature) you offer the respondent a physical copy of the book, for just a small P&P charge (there is a reason for this, and I will explain this in just a moment).

This then takes them to the confirm page (again, make sure your lead site software can provide you with this), and either end the transaction there, or if you wish, offer another up-sell.

With this strategy, you not only get the prospect's name and email address, but hopefully, if your book is of significant value and the offer is well written, you will get a high percentage of respondents' physical mailing addresses too (in order for you to send them the book) not to mention the small P&P cost. It may not seem like a lot of money, most P&P contributions are around the £2.97 mark, but it serves 2 important purposes;

→ It covers the cost of printing the book

→ It gets rid of tyre kickers (people just wanting something for free) and they are trusting you with their credit card details.

Of course there is one downfall with this strategy, but I've already covered the main way to overcome it, and that is, offering a free book attracts the interest of 'freebie seekers'. A large majority of people who request your 'free' book will be just that, freebie seekers, who have no intention of either, a) reading it, and b) taking advantage of the 'call to action' your book sets up.

However, the prospects who go on to buy the book (or at least pay the P&P) are much more targeted, as they have not only done one more step than the free download customers, but also trusted you enough, to give you their credit card details, and you will probably find that it's these customers that will go on to do business with you.

One of my clients – Andrew Ludlam, author of Maverick Marketing (available at www.maverickmarketingconsultancy.co.uk) used this tactic, and here is his experience of how it's worked for him:

"I've always maintained that the best way to engage and develop integrity with your audience is by offering a massive education up front. So when writing Maverick Marketing, my aim from the very start, was to connect and build credibility with my target audience and position myself as an expert – as opposed to 'selling books'.

The approach I used was to create a compelling direct response advert that offered my book as a free PDF download. I then ran this advert in a specific publication that I knew my prospects would read. The advert directed readers to a specific page on my website, where they were able to 'claim' my book. I then subsequently offered the paperback version of Maverick Marketing at a specially discounted rate.

With regard to promoting your book, I would advise testing different approaches with the format of your book and the price point. Find an approach that works best for you, and that your audience is most receptive to.

Whatever approach you choose to use, ultimately writing and publishing your own book is the perfect way to position yourself as an expert in your respective field and gain instant credibility."

2. Free download with first 2 chapters – with the opportunity to buy the full book for full (or discounted) amount.

This is a slight twist on the first strategy, and probably best used with a book that is more of a manual or more in depth 'how to' guide.

Most books I help business owners write are books that outline a problem, and then offer the solution with the 'call to action' (the book doesn't give the full solution, the 'call to action' follow-up does). However there are books that are not just an 'agitator' of a challenge, instead they are a full blown 'How to...' book – which gives all the answers. And it's this type of book, which works well with this tactic (and the next one as well).

The strategy is the same as above, but instead of giving access to the full book as a download, the respondent gets the first few chapters instead, or perhaps the introduction and the first chapter, whichever you think will whet the appetite for the reader to then purchase the rest of the book.

The book can then be offered at either the full price, or you could make a special offer for a limited time, whichever way you choose is up to you.

Another one of my clients – Tim Wareing, author of Toddler Soccer and 1 on 1 Coaching (available at www.ToddlerSoccer.Org/book and www.CoachTim.Org/book) used this strategy, and I know he got a fantastic response:

"When we finished the book, we then offered this option as a free download; the front cover, contents, introduction and 2 free samples of training exercises. This was just to give the potential buyer a feel of the book and what it was we were offering.

At the same time, we had a follow up email that went out to these responders, saying that their request for this free download had been received, and then instructed them to go to a specific landing page where they could purchase the full book (either as an e-book, or a physical copy – both priced accordingly). We also made a premium service available, which included the book along with a private one-on-one session with myself (a recorded conversation over the phone).

Now the e-book sold the most (for both books Toddler Soccer and 1 on 1 Coaching) about 5-1 to the paperback version. But I think that because our books were both 'How to' books people wanted this information on their mobile devices, like i-phone, Blackberry and Kindle. Our prospects were wanting the information instantly so they wanted it in electronic format. I also think that if I hadn't offered the free teaser, people wouldn't have been able to get a feel for the book. When you walk into a bookshop, you can pick up a book, take a look inside, and see the contents, this then all helps with the buying decision. Being on line, you don't have the opportunity to do that, so by offering the first few pages for free, you give them the opportunity to 'try before they buy' and I'm convinced this is why we sold so many copies.

By showing them the contents, the prospect was able to see just how comprehensive the book was. In fact, our conversion rate from free download to purchasing the full e-book was 60% - which is a great response. The remaining 40% we market too, as we now have their email addresses, and we can follow them up with an auto-responder sequence, which then hopefully leads them to buy the full book.

Using this tactic has been incredibly successful for us, and the sequence we used was easy to set up and is now all automated, so I don't have to do a thing. Feel free to visit www.ToddlerSoccer.Org/book to see the sequence. "

Update: Tim has gone on to write two more books, and he is now selling them in over 20 countries. I'm really pleased he's done so well, and his strategy has proved super powerful.

3. Free download of the contents (like the 'look inside' feature on Amazon.com) – with an opportunity to get either the full PDF download or the physical book.

Now this is the strategy I recommend the least, purely because it's the one that gets the least response, and with all the offers of free books out there it's quite a risky tactic. But if you are a well-known author, or of very high standing within your niched area, then offering your book for the full price (or discount) could promise a good response.

However, having said that, the person I first worked for used this tactic, and sold many copies of his book. He offered the contents for free (by running a small ad in the business section of a national paper) which were then mailed to the responder and then emailed and mailed with an offer to buy the book at full price.

The book, now sadly out of print (and the author now out of the Business Sector) worked brilliantly as a stepping-stone for his consulting and seminars. But it's a bold strategy, and doesn't always work.

My colleague and friend, Hollie Gomez, who authored her first book 'The Superstar Staff Solution' (available at www.super-starstaff.com) back in 2010, used this strategy and went on to promote her book in the FSB magazine, offering her book for full price. Unfortunately the campaign did little in terms of revenue (very few responders) and she is now finding that offering the book free on the front end much more profitable.

Which Strategy to Use?

So, I have shared with you the three strategies that I have had experience with. There is no reason why you can't come up with a strategy of your own, but whatever strategy you choose, remember to track your responses, and if at all possible, test your offers.

All I can be certain of is, that using your book as a lead generation tool (the thing that is being offered in exchange for a name and email address) is one of the easiest and simplest strategies a business owner can adopt, and one I would recommend to any 'want to be author'.

The info graphic over the page covers how to get your book marketed once you have your lead page set up. You can download it from www.compass-publishing.com - it's right on the home page.

7 EFFECTIVE WAYS TO GET
YOUR BOOK MARKETED & SOLD
www.thebookrefinery.com

2. Your List
Building up a list of people who want to buy your book is super smart. These are people who have done business with you, know you and trust you. They are your first group to market your book too. Don't have a list? Then follow the next 5 steps and start building.

3. Publications
Which publications do your target audience read? If you can identify that, then test a small add in that publication. Get in contact with the editor of your target magazine and offer a reader offer. See if you can feature in an article. Only spend what you can lose.

4. Book Launch
Get the most leverage out of your book launch. Offer a mini seminar and have guest speakers that will be of benefit to your guests. Don't just have a launch that is all about the book, make it a valuable and memorable to your guests. Invite the press or local radio.

1.
Create a **landing page**. This is where you will direct ALL of your sales. Make it a clean, easy to follow process. Have a **buy it now** button and use a trusted payment method.

WWW.YOURBOOKTITLE.COM
Try and get your book title URL or the closest version This will help promote your book and become the brand. Direct all your advertising to that url. Have an email capture form in the selling process, so you can up-sell any additional products.

5. Social Media
This is great if you have a good following, but remember likes do not mean sales. Direct your followers to your landing page and build good report with them. Offer free info & strong reasons to buy. Remember your competing with 1,000's of other authors, doing the same.

6. Radio
Approach your local radio & offer to speak about your subject. You could have a question & answer session with listeners, but make it ALL about the radio station, rather than you. Give free advice & then you can offer a special deal to listeners of the station.

7. Affiliates/S.A.
Approaching people who offer parallel services to your own can be very effective. You could set up a joint alliance with several non competing companies and offer them a special deal that is just for their customers, in return you get a new stream of targeted leads.

BEWARE - Most newly published authors want to get their book on Amazon. But a few words of caution. Firstly, they charge a high % for the privilege. Do the math before you commit. Secondly, you have NO idea who is buying your book, so if you want to keep a track of your buyers, therefore, sell directly from your landing page.

Figure 4 - Infographic on how to market your book

Summary

Here I've shared a very brief outline on how to market your book with you. There are tons of other information out there on 'book marketing' and I suggest you take a look at all avenues available.

I have found LinkedIn to be a very valuable resource, and there are lots of book marketing groups on there that share some great information and ideas. You can join LinkedIn by visiting www.linkedIn.com.

I haven't included social media in my suggestions, as that could be another book entirely. There are so many different options out there; it's impossible to cover them all in this particular book. However the more ways you get the 'word' out into your market place the better.

Your list (if you have one) will of course be a great place to start, but if this book is to get NEW prospects onto your list, then you will need to find out where your readers 'are', then advertise there.

Whichever avenue you choose, I wish you all the best. Becoming a published author is one of the smartest marketing moves you can make, and you will be viewed as an 'expert' quicker than any other marketing strategy.

I look forward to seeing your book printed and sold, and getting you more clients!

Conclusion

I hope by reading this book you have not only seen the importance and leverage you gain by identifying your niche, but also how becoming an author, can position you as an industry expert within your coaching practice.

I can't recommend strongly enough that you write a book and set yourself up as an 'Expert' in your field. Writing and publishing your book really is a great way to make you stand out from the crowd, and it does this in a way that no other strategy can achieve.

Yes, there's a lot to do and consider, but don't forget that much of this process can be delegated to other people or companies. Don't forget, you now have the entire process explained to you, so you should be able to make an informed decision on which strategy to use.

If you have an idea for a book, or you have a dozen (or more) pages sitting on your hard drive, and you're not quite sure of what to do next, then simply visit www.TheBookRefinery.com and visit the Planning and coaching page, I have several options for you, from a book discovery call, to getting your blueprint plan sorted and of course full coaching solutions. You will see an enquiry form that you can fill out, or simply email me alexa@thebookrefinery.com and tell me a bit about your project. Having over ten years' worth of experience working with business owners, helping them write their books for lead generation, I would be delighted to talk you through your ideas for your publication.

Or if you want to try it yourself, just follow the steps I've outlined and get writing. I look forward to seeing your book being published on sites like Amazon, as well as being used in your marketing strategy to get more customers and clients into your sales funnel.

Start that 'Blueprint Plan' NOW!

Wishing you all the best in your writing,

Alexa Whitten, *your book coach*

You can find me on social media...

Facebook - facebook.com/gettingyourbookpublished

Twitter - @yourbookcoach

Instagram - instagram/Book_coachUK

Special offer

Special offer to readers of 'Publish Your Way to More Clients'

I know it can be hard to get started, and as I have said throughout the book, having help can make all the difference. So I'm offering readers of this book a better than half price deal on my coaching.

Get my unlimited help, (email, phone or skype) for just £150 for the first month. (My monthly coaching is usually £375)

We can brainstorm, plan and get that book written within 12 weeks, and get your book working to attract more paying clients.

With my help you will be able to;

- ✓ Come up with the entire book strategy
- ✓ Help brainstorm title and contents
- ✓ Keep you on track and motivated
- ✓ Write compelling call to actions so that your book converts readers to high paying clients
- ✓ Convert your book to all formats, such as Kindle and PDF
- ✓ Plus much, much more….

So get in touch and quote '*Get Published*' for your better than half price coaching deal. Simply email me at alexa@thebookrefinery.com putting 'Get Published' in the subject line, and I will be in touch to secure your place.

Just think, in less than 12 weeks you too could be a published author – and selling your book on Amazon!

But hurry, this is a limited time offer…I will only be able to take on a limited number of clients at this special rate – once the places have been filled, then the price goes back to £375 a month. So email me now, and secure your place.

About the Author

Alexa started her business in 2009, when her then boss encouraged his clients to write books for Lead Gen. In one particular seminar, a client produced his book with great pride but it was absolutely terrible. The layout was all wrong, the font was not consistent, and page numbers appeared on the inside margins - and this sparked an idea.

Alexa saw a gap in the market and decided to run a parallel company (with her boss's approval) which helped business owners write and typeset books. She then added a coaching arm to her business, and also set up Compass-Publishing which helps authors publish their books as well.

She lives in Portsmouth with her son Oliver, and spends time visiting family and friends in Canada, where she will be returning (she lived there from 1990 -2000) once Oliver starts Uni.

She is a keen sailor (hence the name Compass-Publishing) and skier, and enjoys spending time with friends, enjoying wine and eating out.

She is also passionate about helping people become authors - and loves nothing more than seeing books come to life, especially the printed product.

Acknowledgements

There are so many people to thank - from my mentor and colleague Ed Rivis, who really encouraged me to set out on my own, to Alison Ward who really pushed me to get this book 'out there'.

My son Oliver who always makes me smile, Paul who always patiently reads my blog posts and gives me honest feedback. Keith for reading this book through in its entirety and giving me feedback (and corrections), Danielle who is my partner in crime in getting books edited and ready for publication, and Lisa and David Blann for their encouragement and support. To all my friends and family near and far... you guys are all so fabulous.

Of course, I couldn't not thank my Mum and Dad for their never ending help and praise - sometimes being so far away is hard, but thank God for telephones.

And also, my loyal supporters on Facebook and instagram - it's amazing how a comforting word here, or a like there really helps you keep going - and how can I not forget my clients?... you are all truly amazing people, and there isn't one whom I haven't really enjoyed working with - Good for you, for getting yourself published.

And for all those wanting to write a book... *just do it!*